KING!

PROTEUS BOOKS is an imprint of
The Proteus Publishing Group

United States
PROTEUS PUBLISHING
COMPANY, Inc.
9 West 57th Street, Suite 4503,
New York NY 10019

distributed by:
CHERRY LANE BOOKS
COMPANY, Inc,
P O Box No 430
Port Chester, NY 10573

United Kingdom
PROTEUS BOOKS LIMITED
Bremar House, Sale Place,
London, W2 1PT

ISBN 0 86276 205 7 (Paperback)
ISBN 0 86276 206 5 (Hardback)

First published in U.S. 1985
First published in U.K. 1985

Copyright © 1985 Proteus Books Ltd & Pete Nelson

Photographs courtesy of The Elvisly Yours Collection,
P.O. Box 314, London NW10;
The Rob Burt Collection, Pete Nelson and Wide World Photos.

All rights reserved. No part of this book may be reproduced in any form or by any electronic or mechanical means including information storage and retrieval systems without permission in writing from the Publisher, except by a reviewer who may quote brief passages in a review.

Editor: Mike Brecher

Designed by: The Fish Family
Typeset by: Communitype, Wigston, Leicester

Printed and bound by Cayfosa,
Barcelona, Spain Dep. leg. B-41091 - 1984

NEW TITLES
IN THE PROTEUS ROCKS SERIES:–

A-Z OF ROCK SINGERS; PAT BENATAR; DEF LEPPARD; DURAN DURAN: THE BOOK; FLEETWOOD MAC; MARVIN GAYE; GENESIS; HEAVY METAL BOOTLEG; MICHAEL JACKSON; ELTON JOHN; KING! (ELVIS PRESLEY); LED ZEPPELIN: THE BOOK; LED ZEPPELIN: THE ROAD ALBUM; THE COMPLETE LEPPARD; McCARTNEY; MOTHER! IS THE STORY OF FRANK ZAPPA; THE MOTOWN STORY; OZZY OSBOURNE; POP QUIZ VOL 2; PRINCE; ROCK HERITAGE; THE SIXTIES; ROCKIN' ALL OVER THE WORLD (STATUS QUO); SATISFACTION (MICK JAGGER); BRUCE SPRINGSTEEN: NO SURRENDER; THE STONES BOOTLEG; VAN HALEN

KING!
WHEN ELVIS ROCKED THE WORLD
PETE NELSON

PROTEUS BOOKS
LONDON/NEW YORK

CONTENTS

Chapter One — 9

Chapter Two — 16

Chapter Three — 19

Chapter Four — 40

Chapter Five — 67

Chapter Six — 98

Epilogue — 105

Appendix 1 — 106

Appendix 2 — 108

Chronology — 111

AUTHOR'S NOTE

In the middle fifties, American popular music faced a revolution which was to take Tin Pan Alley by storm. Within a few months the nation's teenagers were to discover not only a new sound, but a new way of life.

Inside two years the music overran America and spread to Britain and Europe. Eventually the entire world would be engulfed, and there would hardly be a citizen of any country on Earth who did not know the name of the young American singer who had been the vanguard of this new music.

His name was Elvis Presley.

The music which was to bring a new kind of freedom as well as pleasure to the world's youth was given many names at first; 'race music' (another name for black artistes music), 'rockabilly' (a fusion of country and black music), and 'rhythm and blues' (black music again), were just a few, but it would eventually become known universally as 'Rock 'n' Roll'.

Many reasons have been given for the upsurge of rock 'n' roll in the fifties, but without a doubt, the biggest single influence was Elvis Presley. It was Presley's naive mixing of his gospel roots with his country and black music influences, which were to form the basis of his unique style.

Even with today's potpourri of musical styles, it is amazing how many singers and musicians can still trace their influences either directly or indirectly back a quarter century to Presley in his greatest years. In the last years of his life, the seventies, he developed another style of presentation which was as popular as anything he had done in the past, and again he influenced many; but in common with most of his longest-standing fans and many of the giants of rock music that followed him, I believe that Elvis Presley's biggest contribution to popular music was made during the period from when he cut his first record up until he joined the Army for National Service, the period between 1954 and 1958. Little more than four years in which Presley and his music literally changed our daily lives. It is, therefore, that particular period on which I have chosen to concentrate in this book; a time when Presley was at his freshest, most innovative, a time when people cared more about the King's latest musical direction than his private life, about which so much has been said and written since his death.

In an effort to recreate those early days of rock 'n' roll as vividly as possible, I have taken the liberty of using dialogue occasionally even though I cannot vouch for the accuracy of every word. I would like to thank everyone who knew the emerging Elvis, were present at the birth down south of rock and were happy to relive that thrilling time with me; especially J. D. Sumner, Carl Perkins and Jerry Lee Lewis, who helped rebuild incidents and snatches of dialogue that bring it all back to life.

Pete Nelson, May '84.

Chapter One

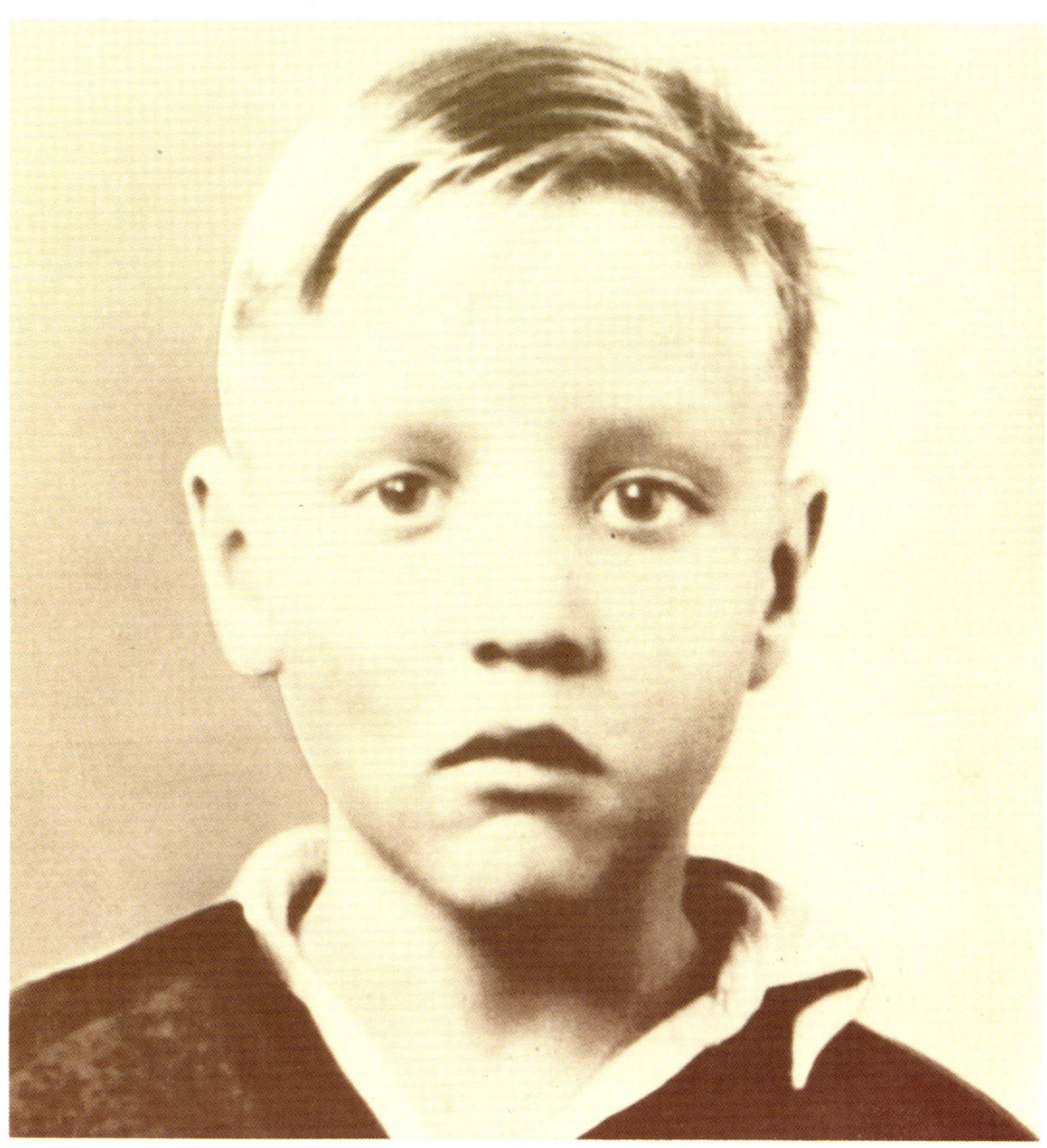

It was a Saturday afternoon in Memphis, the year was 1953, and it was hot. A dusty Ford pickup truck pulled up outside 706, Union Avenue, the young driver grabbed the guitar which was lying on the passenger seat, and entered the building, pausing only to say 'Hi' to the black man lounging against the wall of the premises, which carried a sign over the door proclaiming 'Memphis Recording Service.'

Inside, the young man entered an office, which was occupied by just one person, a woman, who barely looked up when the new arrival coughed nervously, standing by her desk. 'Yes?' the woman finally asked. The young man explained that he would like to make a private recording as a present for his mother. 'You will have to wait your turn,' the woman replied, taking his four dollars and indicating an office full of people, all waiting to make their own private recordings. The youngster indicated that it was okay and sat down with his guitar.

After about twenty minutes, the woman looked up and asked what kind of record did he want to make?

'I'm a singer,' he replied.

'What kind of singer?'

'I sing all kinds.'

The woman smiled. 'Yes, but who do you sound like?' she asked.

'I don't sound like nobody.'

She realized he wasn't the greatest at making polite conversation.

'Do you sing hillbilly?'

Again the reply: 'I don't sound like nobody.'

At that particular time in 1953, no one would have recognized the significance of that remark, even though the man making it was the young Elvis Presley.

Elvis Aaron Presley knew from way back that he wanted to be a singer. His earliest exposure to music was at the small Assembly Of God Church in Tupelo, the town of his birth; his mother has been quoted many times as saying: 'When Elvis was just a little fellow, he would slide off my lap, run down the aisle and scramble up to the platform of the Church. He would stand looking up at the choir and try to sing with them. He was too little to know the words, of course, but he could carry the tune.' As he got older he would sing with his parents at various Church functions, gaining a great liking for gospel singing, and gospel music in general, a liking he was to retain all his life. It was at these Church gatherings that he got his first glimpse of 'showmanship', and it left an indelible mark on the young Presley mind. 'We used to go to these religious singin's all the time. There were these singers, perfectly fine singers, but nobody responded to them. Then there was the preachers, and they cut up all over the place, jumpin' on the piano, movin' every which way. The audience liked 'em, and I learned from them.'

Elvis' first attempts trying to get a singing job came through hanging around the male gospel quartets which were very popular in the South. Groups like The Blackwood Brothers, who used to give concerts every month in Memphis. It was at one of these concerts that J. D. Sumner, the bass singer with the group, first spoke to the gangling youth from Mississippi. 'Kid, I've seen you around here nearly every time we've played Memphis, what's your name?'

Elvis was embarrassed at being spoken to by a 'star' and managed to stammer out: 'Elvis Presley, Mr. Sumner, Sir.'

'Do you like gospel singing?' inquired the deep voiced singer.

'Yessir, and I've been trying all over the place to join a gospel quartet; I wanna be a bass singer like you.'

It was true, Elvis had auditioned for a number of the local gospel groups, and had been turned down. 'You sing too high, Elvis', and 'We don't want nobody singing with us that dresses like a nigger', were just a couple of the common rejections he received. Eventually he was accepted by a group called The Songfellows, who were a junior version of The Blackwood Brothers, but at the last moment the boy who he was to replace in the group changed his mind about leaving and stayed on, so Elvis never actually made the ranks of the gospel quartets. Though he never found an entrée into the gospel mainstream, the black evangelical sound was always close to his heart and, together with the urban blues which put the bite into Presley's delivery it was the biggest influence on his vocal style, an influence which even a decade of crooning his way through pop movies and then another serenading Las Vegas show audiences could not erase.

Memphis Recording Service was housed in a small building which had once been a radiator repair shop; the business was owned by Sam Phillips, the son of a plantation owner. Sam had been heavily influenced by black singers in his youth and, in later life while working as a radio announcer, he realized that while black musicians and singers had a lot to offer musically, they had nowhere to record, so he formed Sun Records and Memphis Recording Service in 1950. The first cuts made for Sun were by artists the likes of B. B. King, Howlin' Wolf (Chester Burnett), Jackie Brenston, and Rosco Gordon.

It was, however, the Memphis Recording Service side of the enterprise which was the most successful at the time. Its motto was 'A complete service to fill every need', and the studio boasted that it was 'combining the newest and best equipment with the latest and finest sonocoustic studios'. Anyone could walk in off the street, and for four dollars

ELVIS

record two sides of a ten-inch acetate which they kept. It was this prospect that brought an eighteen-year-old Memphis electrician/driver to the Union Avenue studios in the fall of 1953.

Marion Keisker was Sam Phillips' office manager, and as she set up the recording for the young truck driver, she studied the lean features, sensuous lips, and lank greased hair combed into a quiff, as the singer stood there clutching the battered guitar on which he accompanied himself. Halfway through his rendition of *My Happiness* something struck a responsive chord in Marion Keisker — something made her tape the last half of that song, and the whole of the next one, *That's When Your Heartaches Begin*. Today she says it was Sam Phillips' words which she remembered; Sam had said: 'If I could find a white man who had the negro sound and the negro feel, I could make a billion dollars.' Marion believes she sensed that in this young man was that 'feel' that Sam was looking for. To her everlasting credit, Marion Keisker put the tape to one side, scribbled a note with it which read: 'Elvis Pressley — good ballad singer — hold'.

'Sam, did you listen to that tape of the Presley kid yet?'

Sam Phillips looked up from the sandwich he was eating, and stared out of the window, 'Yeah, Marion, I listened. The kid's okay. Maybe I'll call him sometime.'

Sam and Marion were sitting in the third booth by the window in Miss Taylor's Cafe, which was situated on the corner of Union Avenue, very conveniently next door to the Memphis Recording Service building. Most of Sam's business seemed to be conducted in the cafe, and that day was no exception; he was kicking around ideas, looking for someone to record, when Marion reminded him of the tape. 'Maybe I'll ask the kid back to the studio,' Sam went on, but it was obvious to Marion that he wasn't really interested at this particular time.

It was to be January 4, 1954, four days before his nineteenth birthday, when Elvis Presley — with one 's' — took the second step towards his destiny. Again he parked the Ford pickup on a parking lot down the street, and walked into the studio on Union Avenue. This time Marion was out, but Sam Phillips was in.

'Hi, I'm Elvis Presley, ah, did Miss Keisker mention me?'

Sam nodded, and said that she had. 'I've also listened to the tape, and you're not bad kid, but I can't use you right at this time'.

Elvis was disappointed, but didn't show it. 'W-w-w-ell okay, Mr. Phillips, but I'd like to make another personal record please.' Sam took the four dollars and set up the primitive single track recording equipment. Elvis sang *Casual Love* and *I'll Never Stand In Your Way*. Before he left Sam again took note of Elvis' address and a telephone number where he could be contacted. 'I'll give you a call sometime,' was Sam's parting remark.

The time had moved on to April 1954, and Sam Phillips had a problem. 'Marion, who is the singer on this demo?' he asked, indicating an acetate which contained a song called *Without You*.

'I don't know Sam, it's just a demo that came in from Nashville, I think they were trying to sell the song rather than the singer.'

Hell! Sam was interested in the song AND the singer. 'Well if we can't trace him, I'm just gonna have to put out the record with somebody else singing the song.'

Immediately Marion went to her files and took out Elvis' address and phone number. 'How 'bout the kid with the sideburns?' She'd put in a word for Presley so many times that she had lost count, but this time her boss listened.

'Okay, if you can get him over here.'

Marion called the number which Elvis had left; it turned out to be a neighbor's house. The neighbor passed on the message and, as Marion says: 'It seemed like I still had the phone in my hand from calling him when he came through the door panting.'

Elvis' first serious session was a disaster. 'Will you sing it like the demo?' Sam kept pleading, trying to get Elvis to copy the vocal sound on the acetate.

Elvis had run through the song a hundred times. 'But Mr. Phillips, it ain't my kinda song.'

'Well, what else ya got?' Sam snapped, by now becoming seriously annoyed.

'I can do anything,' was Elvis' reply.

'Go ahead,' said Sam, 'let's hear it.'

For the next hour Elvis just played and sang snatches from anything he remotely knew — pop, country, R&B, gospel, any-

KING

Elvis and his parents in '55

thing, including a generous selection of Dean Martin material. Elvis had figured that if they wanted him to sound like someone else, it may as well be Dean Martin. Sam Phillips was still not impressed, but said that he could probably find some musicians who could help Elvis, give him a little practise, work a while with him.

Sam called a twenty-one-year-old guitar player called Scotty Moore. Many people, including Sam Phillips, state that it was this guitarist who was responsible more than anyone else for the early 'Elvis Presley rockabilly sound', or as it is now more correctly known, 'the Scotty Moore sound'. In later years, many young guitarists copied or tried to copy Scotty's style and technique. Some succeeded, others not, but after all these years it still remains Scotty's sound.

John Fogerty, erstwhile leader and guitarist of Creedence Clearwater Revival, who had many giant hits in the late sixties and early seventies, cites Scotty Moore's guitar work as the inspiration for their biggest hit *Bad Moon Rising*. Alvin Lee, leader and lead guitarist with British group Ten Years After, who achieved world-wide fame via their appearance at the Woodstock festival in 1969, is quoted as likening Scotty's opening chords on the second lead break on the recording of *Hound Dog* to 'someone dropping a load of scaffolding poles!'. Not the most obvious compliment perhaps, but actually a tribute to the man's unique sound and phrasing, and brilliant inventive quality, a quality which was to be invaluable in creating the hit sounds of those early Elvis recordings on the Sun record label and beyond, right up until Scotty's eventual split with Elvis.

Far Right: **Together with James Dean, Elvis Created the image of raw and restless youth.**

Chapter Two

A long, hawk-like face, sporting a thin Roman nose, hunched over a big semi-acoustic Gibson guitar. Every now and then a semblance of a smile flickers across his face as he watches the antics of the singer in front of him.

Winfield Scott Moore III, or 'Scotty' Moore as he was better known, became a familiar sight on Elvis Presley's live performances in the fifties, and it was hard to imagine Elvis in the early years without Scotty, or for that matter, Bill Black. Scotty Moore's career did not start with the emergence of Elvis Presley, although one could be forgiven for thinking it did.

Scotty was born on December 27, 1931 in Gadsen, Tennessee into a musical family; his father and three elder brothers played together in a country group. In that kind of company it would have been surprising if he had NOT drifted towards the guitar. He in fact started playing at the age of eight, and made great progress, partly due to the fact, he says, that he was left out of the family band, which only acted as a spur to him, and made him practise all the more.

Scotty states that his entry into the navy at the age of sixteen was his big musical turning point. He began listening to the likes of Tal Farlow and Barney Kessel, very influential jazz guitarists, while country guitarists Chet Atkins and Merle Travis also helped shape his early style.

Scotty played with a small band in the navy, and he also did a little broadcasting, but that was the extent of his musical career until he was discharged from the service in 1952. On quitting the navy he started playing with bar bands, the type of bands whose repertoire consisted of 'drinking and fighting music' — country music which for the most part was played to the accompaniment of fist and bottle fights, but if it was played with enough speed and beat it could usually keep the audience's attention, for a while at least. It was here that Scotty learned to fit his licks in with the 'boogie' styled numbers that the bands were performing.

Scotty was performing in and around Memphis now, because on his release from the Navy he fancied the city life rather than going back to the family farm, and as his brother owned a hat business in Memphis, he started to learn the hatter's trade, figuring that people would always want hats.

It was at this point that Scotty put together a band which was to become a very important factor in the Elvis Presley story. The Starlight Wranglers was the band and besides Scotty, it featured Doug Poindexter on vocals, and a tire fitter who worked for Firestone Tires and played upright bass. His name was Bill Black.

The Starlight Wranglers was a country band, very similar to a number of small combos around Memphis and the South at the time, but over a period of a couple of years or so they became quite popular, and Scotty decided that it was perhaps time they made a record. He approached Sam Phillips, but for some while no music was cut as they kicked ideas about. This association led to the two becoming good friends, and eventually a single track was recorded. It was called *My Kind Of Carrying On* written by Scotty. Nearly thirty years later this cut is one of the great rarities of rock history; a mint copy

would be worth a small fortune. The record was cut on June 4 1954, and when it was released, sank without trace.

Scotty's career as a recording artist with Sun would doubtless have begun and ended with *My Kind Of Carrying On* had Sam Phillips not had occasion, during one of his many raps with the boogie guitarist, to mention a nineteen-year-old upstart named Elvis Presley.

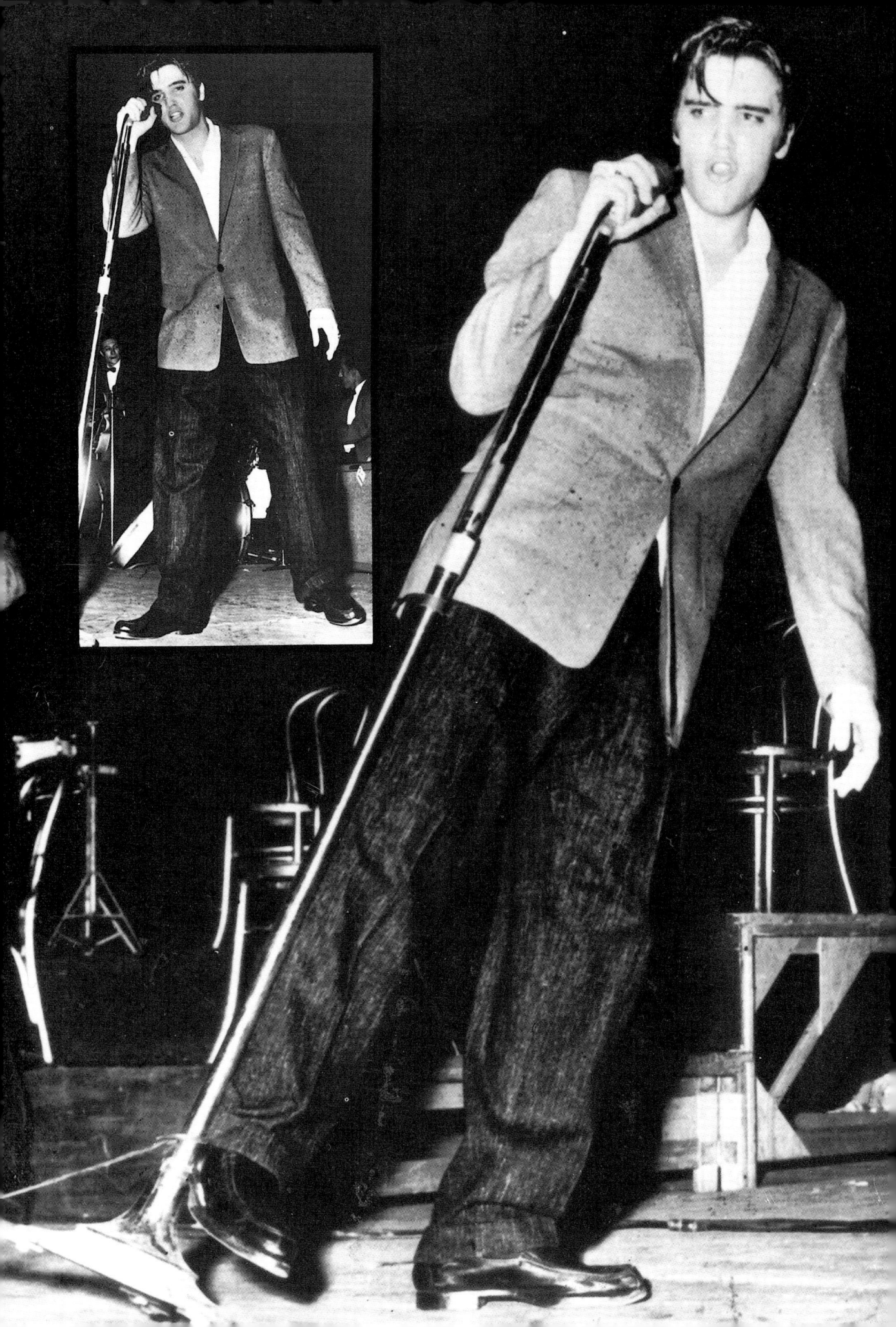

Chapter Three

Sam Phillips fixed up a meeting between Elvis and Scotty Moore; they met at Scotty's house and just sat around playing their guitars, with Elvis singing more or less the same songs and snatches of songs which he had sung for Phillips earlier. Scotty was not very impressed, and said so the next day when he reported back to Sam Phillips. 'Well, the boy's got a good voice, but he didn't do the songs any different or any better than the originals,' was Scotty's appraisal of that first meeting with Elvis. Nevertheless Sam said 'Well, I'll tell you what I'll do, I'll call him and get him into the studio tomorrow, we won't bring in the whole hillbilly group; just you and Bill come in and play a little rhythm, and we'll put some things down, and see what he sounds like coming back off a tape recorder.'

What was to follow was several months of

hard work, rehearsing every day after work to try and capture an acceptable sound. Elvis also worked a few dates with Scotty's band, The Starlight Wranglers, around the local clubs, causing little or no interest at all. General opinion seemed to be that the fuller sound of a band didn't lend itself to Elvis' style at the time. Despite the myth that has grown up around those days at Sun, Elvis was no overnight sensation, simply walking into a recording studio, making a demo record, and being instantly discovered. Indeed, it is difficult to imagine what moved a cool, unimpressed Sam Phillips to persevere with the truck driver, unless perhaps it was the twinge of foresight. Whatever, after months of work, and despite the fact that no one was particularly struck by any of Elvis' performances, Sam Phillips decided at last the time had come to lay down a recording. On July 6, 1954 Elvis sat swigging Coca-Cola straight from the bottle, Bill Black smoked a cigarette, and Scotty Moore plucked idly at the strings of his guitar. The musicians were taking a break after recording *I Love You Because*, an old country and western ballad written and recorded originally by blind singer Leon Payne. Elvis had added a narration in the middle of the tune, similar in style to a recording he had heard by the Inkspots, a group whom Elvis' mother had admired. Strangely, this unedited version of *I Love You Because* was not released until twenty years later.

Suddenly Elvis jumped up, grabbed his acoustic guitar and started leaping about, singing and strumming an old negro blues tune called *That's Alright Little Mama*; Scotty joined in, picking licks on his big semi-acoustic Gibson. Bill, who hadn't yet fully taken to 'this snotty nosed kid' as he called him, took longer to join in, but eventually he picked up on the number, and the three musicians kicked around this old blues tune, which had been written by Arthur 'Big Boy' Crudup.

'What in hell are you doing?' Sam Phillips rapped out the question as he came through from the control room.

'Aw, we were just fooling around Sam,' Scotty replied.

'Well, do it again' was Sam's response, 'but this time do it with the mikes on.'

That's Alright Mama was recorded in a couple of takes, and it was put down 'live', which means it was recorded with Elvis singing and playing rhythm guitar at the same time, while Bill and Scotty accompanied him. Overdubbing was unheard of, let alone in common use, in those days. With one song laid down, it was obvious that another suitable number would have to be found as the flip. After much discussion it was decided to record *Blue Moon Of Kentucky*, a bluegrass tune written and originally performed by the top bluegrass artist of the time, Bill Monroe. Whether this song was chosen purely by chance is a matter of conjecture. It is more likely that it was chosen because of its popularity in country music circles; country was the big selling sound, along with the blues, at the time.

The initial treatment which Elvis gave the tune was that of a straight country ballad, which was different enough as the song was originally done as a country waltz. After the first couple of takes however, Sam Phillips remarked: 'That's fine, hell that's different, that's a pop song now — do it faster.' Elvis, Scotty, and Bill complied, and came up with a classic rocking performance of the song, which is still capable of sending tingles up the spine.

The three musicians crowded into the tiny control room with Sam Phillips to listen to the playback of the two songs. All were in agreement that the sound was exciting, but Scotty expressed some reservations about the reception it was likely to receive from the record-buying public. 'Good God, they'll run us outta town when they hear it!' He was particularly concerned about the fact that they had succeeded in capturing the sound of the black man, but had put it to use on a country song, fusing two very different types of music, and in doing so they had 'invented' a form of music that would be forever known as 'rockabilly'.

It would make a nice story to say that everyone involved in that historic session immediately recognized that a legend was in the making. In truth, none of them felt the earth move. Elvis continued driving a truck for the Memphis firm of Crown Electrics, Scotty and Bill continued concentrating on their band The Starlight Wranglers, Sam Phillips thought that at best *That's Alright Mama* might give Sun a minor hit with the

The King

ELVIS

local radio stations; the big wide world remained blissfully unaware of the existence of one Elvis Presley.

Sam Phillips took the disc round to a white disc jockey with whom he was friendly, Dewey Phillips (no relation to Sam) who had a program on station WHBQ in Memphis called *Red Hot and Blue*, most of which was devoted to black blues singers. It was about the only place he could have gone with the record, for this fusion of black and white music was like poison in the bigoted southern states. Getting any airplay at all was going to take a minor miracle. 'I like the record, Sam,' was Dewey's reaction on listening to the two sides, 'but I guess I'll have to play *That's Alright Mama* 'cause it's more in line with the other stuff on my program, I'll play it tomorrow night.'

At 462 Alabama Street, Elvis Presley tuned the family radio to station WHBQ, then realized he just couldn't sit and listen to his own voice. 'I'm gonna go down to the Suzore, Mom' — meaning the Suzore No.2 Theatre, his favorite haunt — 'I'll see you later, you make sure y'all listen now.'

He had only been at the theatre about an hour when his parents came looking for him. 'Come on, son,' Vernon Presley whispered in the darkness of the cinema. 'Mr. Phillips played your record and all the folks have been ringing the station; he wants to interview you on the radio.' Dewey Phillips had played the record, and the station had been inundated with calls to play it again, and again...and again.

Elvis arrived at the radio station breathless and a little bewildered. 'I don't know nothin' about being interviewed, Mr. Phillips.'

'That's okay,' replied Phillips, 'just don't say nothin' dirty.'

The disc jockey played a couple of records softly in the background. 'Where did you go to school, Elvis?' was the first question he asked.

'Humes High School, sir.' That cleared up the question of Elvis' color; the DJ realized that many of the listeners had assumed Presley was black, but Humes was a white school. After five minutes or so of talk, Phillips wrapped it up with 'All right Elvis, thank you very much.'

'Aren't you gonna interview me?' asked the surprised young man.

'I already have, the mikes have been open all the time!'

Elvis broke out into a cold sweat, but it was over and he had gotten through his first public interview.

Sun Records was taken completely by surprise. The disc that Dewey Phillips had played was only an acetate, (a thin plastic demo disc with a short playing life), and no master pressing had yet been made of the song, but waiting on Sam Phillips' desk were orders for 5,000 copies of the cut, all having been the result of that airing on the radio. The gamble had paid off. The label had played with fire mixing black and white music in the potentially explosive South, but the young people liked it, and they wanted more.

However, to market a singer with a black/white approach nationally was virtually impossible, as Phillips was finding out. The U.S. Government had, only two months earlier, passed a bill outlawing racial segregation in schools, but in those days, and even today to a lesser degree, in the south you were either white or black.

Sun Records, which still consisted of only Sam and Marion Keisker, sent out about 1,000 free copies of the record to disc jockeys with little response. Sam asked the DJs to 'just play the record once', but his pleas fell mainly on deaf ears, or ears deafened by racial and musical prejudice. Black DJs heard *Blue Moon Of Kentucky* and threw the record out, and the country disc jockey didn't want to know, because to them both tracks sounded like black music.

Tom Phillips, Sam's brother, worked for a paper firm, involving him in a great deal of traveling around Tennessee, Mississippi, Louisiana, and his home state of Alabama, and he always carried stocks of Sam's records with him on his travels, calling on radio stations along the way; nearly everywhere he called, the stations gave Tom the Presley record back. Sam Phillips came in for some heavy personal criticism from other luminaries in the recording business. The industry couldn't make up its mind about the young Elvis — some pundits thought he sounded too country for a black singer, others considered he was too black for a country artist. He was certainly 'too' something!

Elvis joined The Starlight Wranglers, and started work with them at the Bel Air Club in Memphis, but almost immediately his

KING

ELVIS KING

A photo that became news: two months before becoming the subject of a notorious custody case, following the death of her parents in an auto accident, a smiling five-year-old Elvis in New Orleans, July '56.

presence within the ensemble created friction. As Scotty Moore recalls: 'Since Bill and I had done the two songs on the record with him, when he'd come on everyone else had to drop out, or it wouldn't have been the record, and so the other guys, rightfully so, were in a 'left out of the spotlight situation'; and so after a few weeks of this everybody agreed that it was not gonna work that way, so the others said, "well you guys go ahead because it looks like you might have something going." But I don't think there was any ill feeling at the time.' The Starlight Wranglers broke up, leaving Scotty and Bill free to work with Elvis, although at the time they were all still holding down full time employment during the day. They decided that any money they made would be split three ways, 25% each for Scotty and Bill, and 50% for Elvis.

July 20, 1954. A flatbed truck, borrowed from a farmer, is parked behind a new drugstore on Lamar Avenue, Memphis; the parking lot is full of inquisitive people watching as the three musicians climb up onto the truck and start to play. It is their first public engagement as a trio, and they are playing at the opening of the drug store. The audience stare in disbelief; 'What's he doing?' and 'Who the hell is he?' are some of the milder questions being asked. A few know the name of Elvis Presley, because they have heard the record on the radio, but the majority can't figure out this energetic young singer wearing a pink shirt, and black pants. They stand and they stare. Eventually a ripple of response starts at the front of the crowd, Bill Black 'riding' the big acoustic bass fiddle as though he were on a horse, clowning and acting the fool. The audience warm to the trio after Bill's attempt at cracking the atmosphere, and at the end of their performance, the teenagers in the crowd are jumping and shouting and generally going crazy.

The trio received a similar reception wherever it appeared in those first weeks; all the venues were in and around Memphis, primitive gigs consisting of High School auditoria, store openings, and guest spots at the Eagles Nest Night Club which was situated on Highway 78.

During this early period, Elvis acquired his first manager, none other than Winfield Scott Moore III. A document was drawn up by a local attorney which read that W. S. Moore III was a 'band leader and booking agent', and Elvis Presley was a 'singer of reputation and renown'. Scotty was to get 10% of all bookings he got the trio; the document was signed by Elvis, Scotty, and both Elvis' parents and was dated July 12, 1954. In August of that year two cars set out from Memphis to make the four hour journey to Nashville. In the first car were Sam Phillips and Marion Keisker; they had closed the Sun Recording Company offices for a couple of days so they could take the time out to visit Nashville with Elvis, Scotty, and Bill, who were to appear on the celebrated 'Grand Ole Opry' radio show.

Since 1925 The Grand Ole Opry in Nashville has been the accepted pinnacle in country music. Everyone who is anyone in country music has appeared on the Opry. It is considered an honor to guest on the show, but the fact that the stars are paid only minimum union rate, that they have to guarantee to appear on a fixed number of Saturday nights, does little to foster a financial incentive to feature on the show. Nevertheless, there has never been a shortage of acts eager to do the Grand Ole Opry, and in 1954 the Opry was most definitely THE place for a new country act to break, much more so perhaps than nowadays. The Opry had become the next step in Sam Phillips' plans for Elvis Presley. The appearance had been arranged by Phillips through a friend, and everyone connected with Elvis and Sun records was excited about the prospect of his being on the nation's most prestigious country show.

Scotty Moore's Chevvy followed Sam's car into Nashville. Scotty, Bill, and Elvis sat together in the front seat, while the rear seat and the luggage boot were taken up by guitars, a small amplifier for Scotty's guitar and some stage clothes, and strapped to the roof of the auto was Bill's big stand-up bass.

'Man, is this the place?' Elvis was visibly taken aback at the sight of the large Ryman Auditorium building which housed the Grand Ole Opry radio show. He stepped out of the car, stuck his hands in his pockets and stared at the shabby black and white frontage. Inside, the three musicians reported to Jim Denny who was responsible for booking the acts on the Opry.

'Howdy fellas, where's the rest of the band?' Denny shook hands looking round for other musicians.

'There's only three of 'em,' Sam replied.

Auditioning for *The Godfather*

'Well shit man, I want the whole band just like the record, you don't come down here shortchanging me.' Denny, furious, had decided he was being conned. 'Our agreement was we were gonna have the performance just like it is on the record.'

It took a while, but eventually Sam convinced him that the only guys who were playing on Elvis' record were standing right there in front of him.

In the afternoon, Elvis took a look around the Ryman Auditorium. The building had been constructed in 1892, originally as a revival tabernacle, but in 1941 the Grand Ole Opry moved in, making Ryman its permanent home. (In the mid-seventies the program was moved to a new custom-built Opry house just outside of Nashville.)

'Is this what I've been dreaming of all my life?' Presley asked Marion, looking round at the hard, church type pews, on which the audience paid to sit, the bare iron radiators dotted around the walls, and the very evident shortage of paint on the walls and stage area. 'Man, I don't believe it,' was all Elvis could say.

In the evening the show was divided into half hour and quarter hour segments, each segment having its own compere. On Elvis' section of the show, Hank Snow was the compere. Hank was one of the most popular of all the Opry acts, and had just had a Number One country hit with *I Don't Hurt Anymore*. Waiting at the side of the stage to go on, Hank turned to Elvis and asked, 'What's your name again?'

'Elvis Presley, sir,' came back the reply.

'No,' said Hank, 'not that, I mean the name you sing under?'

'Elvis Presley, sir,' the young singer reiterated.

Elvis sang *Blue Moon Of Kentucky*, as that was considered the more country of the two songs, and the audience reaction was minimal. They were used to seeing the likes of Hank Snow, Lester Flatt and Roy Acuff, standing still and singing in whining nasal voices, but in Presley was this flashily dressed kid, leaping around the stage singing Bill Monroe's classic song at four times the speed of the original. To say they were not impressed was an understatement.

When the show was finished, Elvis sought out Jim Denny. 'What did you think, Mr. Denny?'

'Well, I'll tell ya kid,' replied Denny. 'If you'll take my advice, you'll stick to drivin' a truck.'

Elvis was shattered, so were Sam and Marion. On the way home in the car, Elvis wept openly. 'Scotty, what did we do to them folks, why didn't they like us?'

'I said all along, Elvis, that we're takin' a chance singin' them songs that way,' replied Scotty. 'But you don't know any other way of doin' 'em... so what the hell.'

Elvis never forgot that night in Nashville, and much later in his career, at a social function, Elvis again met Jim Denny. Throwing his arms around Elvis' shoulder, Denny announced to people around: 'I always knew this boy had it in him to make it.' Elvis responded on cue with a dutiful 'Yes sir, thank you, sir,' then out of the corner of his mouth he said to one of his companions: 'The son-of-a-bitch don't remember when he broke my heart.'

Two months later in October 1954, the disappointment of Nashville was put behind them when Elvis, Scotty, and Bill arrived in Shreveport, Louisiana, to appear on 'The Louisiana Hayride', a radio program which had been started six years earlier in an attempt to cash in on the success of the Opry show. Although it was an infant in comparison with the Opry, the Hayride had already been instrumental in establishing one country star — the legendary Hank Williams. Later, Johnny Cash would be indebted to the Hayride for the boost the show gave his fledgling career. Elvis fared a great deal better on the Hayride than he had in Nashville, which is hardly surprising. Even today, the Opry is a very straight-laced, traditional show, not noted for its enthusiasm for anything new or different. Back in 1954 someone as new and different as Elvis didn't stand a chance.

Elvis chewed his lip, waiting nervously in the Hayride wings. It was his first appearance on the program, and he was a little worried after the fiasco in Nashville.

One of the stars of the show, country singer Johnny Horton, was making conversation with Elvis to help calm his nerves. The announcer, Frank Page's introduction that night was to become a moment of rock 'n' roll history — 'Just a few weeks ago, a young man from Memphis, Tennessee recorded a song on the Sun label and, in just a matter of a few

ELVIS

This was a posed shot taken to counteract some bad publicity Elvis received after a fist fight with two filling station attendants in '56. Elvis is reported to have left one pump boy with a black eye, which didn't hurt his reputation one bit.

KING

weeks, that record has skyrocketed right up the charts. It's really doing well all over the country. He's only nineteen years old, he has a distinctive new style......Elvis Presley!'

Elvis went on and sang *That's Alright Mama*, and was a success. The audience at the Hayride was much younger and broad-minded than the Opry audience, and as such much more tolerant of Elvis' wilder style.

After the show, Horace Logan, the station director for KWKH radio, who ran the Hayride, signed Elvis to a twelve month contract to appear weekly, and to sing some of the station's commercials, for a fee of $18 per show.

Elvis' style of singing at the time was matched by his unorthodox between-songs patter; he was like a machine gun, spilling out words quickly, stammering, and mumbling. His introduction to Chuck Berry's song *Maybelline* went — 'Thank you very much, we gotta song right now friends, that we'd like to do for ya, we ain't been doin' it long, but, but, but, well, we, yeah, we ain't done it but once on the Hayride. We only learned it a couple of days ago, and we'd like to do it for you right now, hope you like the way we do it. It's a song about, uh,...a song about a......a song that goes sumpin' like this.'

The Hayride had seats for about 3,500 people, and just as Hank Williams had done before him, and Johnny Cash would do later, Elvis always filled the place. He was a popular act both on and off stage.

Most of the acts that appeared on the Hayride were booked out together as a package show, and Elvis featured on most of these with artists like Johnny Horton, Faron Young, David Houston, Tillman Franks and Betty Amos. They toured the South Western area of Arkansas, North Louisiana, and East Texas, an area covered by station KWKH and known locally as the 'Ark-La-Tex' area.

The tours were well received, because of the popularity of the radio program, and each artist did no more than a couple of numbers in a fast moving show. On the majority of these packages Elvis was booked as 'The Hillbilly Cat' or 'The King Of Western Bop', and announcer Horace Logan used to refer to him many times as 'The Memphis Flash'.

The trio were now working very regularly at nights, and one day in late '54 Elvis walked nervously into his boss' office at Crown Electrical. James Tipler looked up from the bundle of papers on his desk; he figured he knew what the young man had come to say, but he let Presley stammer: 'Mr Tipler, sir, ahv, ah, ahve just...well, I can't carry on singin' every night and workin' for you, so I gotta...ah...'

Tipler put the about-to-be ex truck driver out of his misery. 'Okay, Elvis, you can finish at the end of the week, you can't carry on the way you are anyway.'

Elvis collected his pay packet at the weekend with mixed feelings, sorry he was leaving, but excited at the thought of becoming a professional singer at last.

A couple of weeks later, Elvis was booked on what was to be his biggest live appearance to date. It was at the Overton Park Shell in Memphis, and the headliners were Marty Robbins and Webb Pierce.

In the afternoon show, Elvis was received only moderately. He had sung a couple of country ballads in keeping with the format of the show. Elvis' old friend Dewey Phillips was watching the show. 'You know, Elvis, you gotta get out there tonight and give 'em some of that boppin' stuff. How 'bout that new record Sam sent me? Sing that.'

Elvis was unsure; 'But it's a country audience, Mr. Phillips, they've come to see Marty, and Webb Pierce.'

However, Phillips persuaded Elvis to sing *Good Rockin' Tonight* at the evening performance, and the audience went wild.

They loved him, and were screaming for more. Elvis passed Webb Pierce as he left the stage, and smiled at the country star. Pierce's reaction was a snarled 'You son-of-a-bitch!' — he was furious, and Elvis discovered for the first time that not every one of his fellow artists was going to be grateful to Presley for changing the course of popular music. Nevertheless, the ex-trucker was about to have a profound effect on both Webb Pierce and Marty Robbins, as both of them started to record 'rockabilly' type material in an effort to cash in on the growing popularity of the new style. In fact it was only three months after this show that Marty Robbins recorded a version of *That's Alright Mama* not a million miles distant in style from Elvis' rendering.

During September 1954, Elvis had returned to Sam Phillips' studio to lay down another two songs for a follow-up single and in

Main photo: Elvis returns home, at the Mississippi-Alabama State fair, Tupelo, Sept 27, 1956.

October of that year Sam released *Good Rockin' Tonight*[1]— backed with *I Don't Care If The Sun Don't Shine* -. In reviewing the record, Billboard magazine called Elvis 'a sock new singer', and proclaimed that he 'could appeal to both country and R&B fans as well as pop'. However, the record did not sell as well as the first; it reached Number Three in the Memphis charts, but didn't chart in any other markets at all.

Nevertheless, his barely off-the-mark career was about to receive a little recognition. One of the key questions in a national poll of leading disc jockeys was 'Who do you consider the most promising new hillbilly or country and western artist?'
On the strength of just one record release, and a career which had only begun in July of that year, Elvis Presley was voted into eighth place.

It was at the Overton Park Shell concert that Elvis was first approached by Bob Neal. The promoter of the show, Bob knew Elvis from years earlier when he ran a gospel radio show which had featured amongst others, The Blackwood Brothers. 'Elvis, have you got yourself a manager yet?'

Elvis frowned; he had been asked this question so many times recently. 'Well, yeah, Mr. Neal, Scotty's my manager.'

'What kinda shows is he bookin' ya?' Neal asked.

'Well, we've got work all over the place, we've done schoolhouses, and drugstore openings, and...'

'Hold it, Elvis,' Neal cut in.

'Who do ya think booked ya into this show today?' Before Elvis could answer, Neal continued: 'I did, and I know that it's the biggest show you've done to date.'

It was true, and Elvis knew it. Bob Neal got Scotty and Elvis together, and they worked out a deal. Neal would act as manager and booking agent for 20% of their earnings, while Scotty and Bill would be put on a salary plus 1% of all record sales.[3]

Scotty didn't mind giving away Elvis' contract, as he knew it was going to the right man. He told Elvis: 'There are gonna be things which you are gonna be involved with, that me and Bill won't; so it wouldn't be fair if me and Bill was on a percentage of your earnings.'

The move was shrewd, a logical one for Elvis at this stage of his career, for Bob Neal was at the time more of a celebrity in the mid South than Elvis was. He had a morning show on WMPS radio in Memphis, on which he played music, chatted, and told jokes.

He also staged shows locally, such as the one at the Overton Park Shell, which he could publicize heavily on his radio program. Neal would book a schoolhouse, or a college auditorium, and would compere the show himself; oftentimes he was responsible for taking the money on the door too! In fact, it was usually the appearance of Bob Neal that was responsible for drawing the gate, though pretty soon after Neal and Elvis teamed up, the DJ/promoter found that his 'boy' was doing all the drawing necessary.

Elvis, Scotty and Bill were still traveling to all their gigs in Scotty's 1954 Chevrolet Bel Air; often enough they slept in the car, and often enough the auto broke down on rough unmade back roads, but they kept it going — they had to! The trio's career was beginning to go; the boys had to travel every week to Shreveport to appear on the Hayride, and in between, the flow of one-nighters was becoming a flood. Sandwiched between all the time on the road, Elvis had to find time to make another recording session.

December 1954, and Elvis, Scotty and Bill were back in Sam Phillips' studio on Union

Arriving for a gig on the Canadian tour

Avenue, Memphis. With them was another musician, drummer D. J. Fontana, the staff drummer on Louisiana Hayride. Fontana had become very friendly with the trio during their appearances on the Hayride, and had worked with them on the Hayride package shows. His particular style of drumming was complementary to Elvis' style, and he soon worked up a musical rapport with the singer.

At the studio Sam was taking his protégé to task. 'But Elvis, you should have gotten something ready to record. Can't you think of anything?'

'But Sam, we've been having such a heavy time on the road, I ain't had time to learn nuthin' new,' replied the eager-to-please Elvis.

'Well, what you got then, anything at all ya bin singin' on the road?'

It was Bill who suggested a song: 'What about that country thing we've bin doin', Elvis? *You're A Heartbreaker*.' 'Yeah, that's a good one,' was Elvis' curt reply. Actually, it wasn't that great; a typical country song, fairly pedestrian in its original format, but as usual the boys gave it more of an uptempo treatment, with drummer D. J. Fontana adding to the beat.

While they felt in that particular mood, they put down another country song, *I'm Left, You're Right, She's Gone*, written by steel guitarist Stan Kesler.

The session had almost come to an end; D. J. Fontana had in fact already left the studio, and Elvis sat idly strumming his guitar, singing snatches of old blues tunes, one of which was *Milk Cow Blues*, an old Sleepy John Estes tune which Estes had originally recorded in 1930 [4]   He sang through a couple of verses, and as usual Scotty and Bill joined in. Again it was Bill who had suggested it. 'Hey, how 'bout doin' a blues tune, Elvis?'

'Hell no man, it don't move,' was Elvis' reply.

'Well, let's move it then,' screamed Bill, and started his usual clowning with the big acoustic bass fiddle, riding it, and dancing with it around the tiny studio.

Elvis screwed up the piece of paper he had picked up, and playfully tossed it at Bill. 'Man, you're squirrely,' Elvis laughed, 'but maybe you've got something there.'

The three musicians went through the song at a fast pace, and were pleased with the result. Then Sam Phillips suggested that Elvis should start the vocal very slowly, stop, and say something like, 'Hey, it don't move.' Presley agreed, and so when the finished version had been recorded it contained a somewhat stilted Elvis saying: 'Hold it, fellas — it don't move me — let's get real gone for a change.'

Elvis' third single was released in January of 1955 and sold very poorly; in fact, in its original form (not counting re-releases) it was just about Elvis' worst selling single.

But by March of 1955 Bob Neal had reason to be excited. 'Great news, fellas, I've got ya an audition with Arthur Godfrey's 'Talent Scouts' show in New York.' His audience of three open-mouthed musicians couldn't believe its luck. The Godfrey program was, at the time, the most important television showcase for new acts.

'Hell, Bob, how we gonna get there?' asked Scotty.

'You're gonna fly, son, and I'm paying.'

At this Elvis looked visibly shaken; Bob noticed the change and reassured Elvis that flying was nothing, that the flight wouldn't take long anyhow.

Elvis hated flying, and he hated New York, particularly a cold and windy March New York, and it showed at the audition. He wasn't too enthusiastic, and gave a less than spirited performance of *Good Rockin' Tonight*. Dispirited or not, the performance was still too wild and too different for the New York talent spotters, who decided they could afford to turn Elvis down.

The following day the boys flew back to Memphis; nothing was ever said again about the failed audition. It obviously hadn't hit them as hard as the infamous Opry appearance.

At this point Elvis was still only appearing as bottom of the bill on most shows he worked. He topped the bill for Bob Neal's presentations, of course, largely because he was the only act on the show, but at the bigger gigs he appeared with the likes of Hank Snow, Faron Young, Slim Whitman, The Wilburn Brothers, Onie Wheeler, and Mother Maybelle and The Carter Sisters, all recognized country acts, who appeared way above Presley on the billing. Not all the acts however were keen to follow Elvis on stage, and only singers such as Hank Snow (at the time the Number One country act) dared follow him. Elvis was beginning to enjoy a sense of power that came from making it tough for the other acts.

Most of these shows were billed as 'The Hank Snow Jamboree' and were booked and promoted by the manager of Hank's production company — Colonel Tom Parker.

It is 26 May, 1955, and Elvis is approaching Meridian, Mississippi for the annual Jimmie Rodgers Memorial celebration. The '54 Cadillac that Elvis has just bought is running sweetly, and Elvis is singing behind the wheel. 'The car sure runs fine, Elvis,' remarks Scotty, 'but for how long?' Scotty is obviously recalling the many cars that the trio had either wrecked or driven into the ground over the past eighteen months of touring. The last one had been a 1951 Lincoln Continental which Bill had wrecked in Arkansas in a collision with a truck.

'Makes no difference,' replies Elvis, 'if this one goes I'll just buy another,' and he smiles to himself, thinking back to when, just a couple of years ago, he wouldn't have been able to afford the hubcaps off a Cadillac. Now he can afford half a dozen cars if he wanted. Man, it makes him feel the most important dude in the States.

Bill's voice brought him out of his daydream. 'There's the Jimmie Rodgers Memorial.' Bill was pointing to a white memorial slab a little larger than a gravestone standing in front of a locomotive and tender. Elvis stopped the car and went over to examine the memorial to the man whose memory they were to honor at the day's performance.

Underneath a carving of Rodgers were the words 'James Charles Rodgers — born Meridian, Miss. September 8, 1897 — died New York May 26, 1933 — The silver tones of his voice, the magic strumming of his guitar, the haunting melody and the heart throbs of his American folk songs brought comfort, joy and inspiration to the millions who heard him on the stage, in broadcasts, and on recordings. Through long years of hardship to the triumphs of his fame, his simple philosophy of life and his devotion to family and friends remains unchanged, because his religion was love — The underest dog is just as good as I am; and I'm just a good as the toppest dog.'

Elvis stood reading the words out loud, and was visibly moved by them; he turned to Scotty and Bill, and said: 'One day I'm gonna be as famous as that.'

The show that night featured Hank Snow, Ernest Tubb and Elvis amongst others, and backstage Tubb was reminiscing on the influence Rodgers had been on his own career, turning to Elvis he said: 'Son, if you become half the singer and entertainer that man was you're gonna do well.'

The Colonel's cue was about to arrive. Tom Parker was an ex-fairground and traveling showman, well versed in the art of leading people where they didn't realize they wanted to go — in some circles they call it 'conning'. Businessman, showman, con-artist, call him what you will, the fact remains he was a shrewd man. At the time he became aware of Elvis, Tom Parker was managing Eddy Arnold, a country music superstar of the time. Arnold put one thing straight about the Colonel when he stated that: 'No matter what, if Tom Parker was your manager, then he was one hundred percent for you and no one else.'

And that, Parker surely proved with Elvis.

Tom Parker's right hand man Oscar Davis was the first to spot Elvis. Presley was appearing at the Airport Inn in Memphis, and Davis was in town setting up a tour for Eddy Arnold. Bob Neal took Davis to see the kid work, and what he saw impressed him enough to report back to the Colonel.

Presley and Colonel Tom moved into each other's orbits little more than a month after Bob Neal had become involved with Elvis. The following week Parker, Elvis, Scotty, Bill and Bob Neal met up in a Memphis coffee shop. Tom Parker sat like a Buddah in an open necked shirt, puffing on his usual cigar, and addressed Bob Neal rather than the three musicians. 'Well, I'll tell ya Bob, if'n I'm gonna do anything with the boy I'll have to get him on a bigger label. Sun Records ain't nuthin'.'

At that, Elvis spoke up. 'Mr. Phillips has been real good to me, there's no reason why I'd wanna leave him.' Scotty and Bill also showed their reluctance to leave Sun, and Bob said he knew that Sam Phillips would not, in any case, be prepared to let Elvis go.

With apparent disinterest Parker left the coffee shop, but true to the form he would display in the decades ahead, Parker had Elvis' potential checked out; record chart placings were researched, the fact that his

contract on the Louisiana Hayride had been extended was noted; so too was the fact that Elvis was despised by the Grand Ole Opry crowd, though this seemed to bother the Colonel little.

On April 1, 1955, Sun Records released Elvis' latest single which coupled the side they had recorded in December with another song which had been recorded in a hurried session in February.

The February session, although rushed, had spawned three tracks, *Baby, Let's Play House* written by black artist Arthur 'Hard Rock' Gunter, *Mystery Train* again written by a black blues singer, Junior Parker, and as was now becoming increasingly common for Elvis, a country song written by Jimmy Wakely, *I'll Never Let You Go*. Sam Phillips chose the rocking *Baby, Let's Play House* as the A side, a tune in which Elvis employed what became one of his more famous vocal gimmicks, the 'hiccupping' sound, in which Elvis tried to imitate the echo on Scotty's guitar. This sound became the butt of many initiative impressions of Elvis, but the fact is he only ever used the technique once, on the *Play House* cut.

On April 5, at Chattanooga, Elvis was working a show with Hank Snow, Ferlin Husky, Jim Ed Brown, and Onie Wheeler. Elvis' parents came to see the show, and struck up a backstage conversation with Tom Parker, the promoter. Said Parker: 'Mrs. Presley, you've a mighty fine boy there, he's gonna be a star, but you know these folks are workin' him too hard.'

At that, Gladys Presley's ears pricked up. For a few months now she had been on at Elvis for working so hard; she'd seen her son come home after a tour whacked, his face coming out in spots from irregular and unhealthy meals taken on the road, and had begged him to slow down. Now she was hearing this man echo her own thoughts. Gladys listened. 'Mrs. Presley, I think your boy needs a good and professional manager who will look after him just as though he was a son.' As always, Parker had done his homework, and knew just how to find Gladys Presley's weak spot.

'I guess you're right, Colonel,' Gladys eventually replied. 'I'll speak to Vernon about it.'

Parker was now well into his stride. 'Well, there's no need to do that Mrs. Presley,' he went on. 'I've already had discussions with Vernon and he said that it was just a matter of talking to you.'

Gladys looked at him warily. 'But even if I give my agreement, Elvis is already signed with Mr. Phillips and Mr. Neal, and those nice people on the radio in Louisiana.'

At this the Colonel threw back his head and chuckled. 'Oh, Ma'am, don't you go worrying yourself over things like that, the old Colonel here has ways and means of getting round those things.'

Gladys left that night not totally convinced; she didn't take a great liking to Colonel Parker, but Vernon assured her that letting Parker handle Elvis' business in the future would be the best for everyone.

Sam Phillips was annoyed. He threw an empty tape box across the studio, bouncing it off the opposite wall. 'Hell, Marion! — that son-of-a-bitch Parker is tryin' to steal Elvis.'

Marion Keisker said nothing, figuring it was best to keep her mouth firmly shut when Sam was in this mood. Sam had just come back from Elvis' home where he had spoken with Vernon Presley. 'You know what Vernon said? He said that my company is nuthin' without his son, and Elvis ain't gonna get nowhere while he's with Sun Records. Now that's Parker's doin', he's bin feedin' Vernon all that bullshit about bein' his manager. Well, all right let him be his manager, let him take Elvis away if he can. I'll sign other singers, I made Elvis a star, so I'll do it again with someone else.'

Marion still kept her council. She believed Sam was right to be mad, believed that Elvis would be making a big mistake if he left Sun, and believed in Sam's ability to find another star bigger than Presley would ever be.

Parker started putting the word around that Elvis' contract was up for sale, and slowly offers started coming through to Sam Phillips. Decca Records' A&R man Owen Bradley turned down the contract when asked $5000, Dot Records also backed out at $7,500, and Mitch Miller, then head of the mighty Columbia Records, was asked $20,000 dollars and retorted: 'No singer is worth that kinda money!'

It was Tom Parker who was responsible eventually for Elvis' move to RCA Records, a move which Parker had intended all along, as both Eddy Arnold and Hank Snow recorded for the label. Arnold Shaw, a New York music publisher was visiting Parker's

Two contrasting faces of Elvis Presley, from the Steve Allen show broadcasts, July 1956.

house during the summer of '55 and Parker persuaded Shaw to listen to a couple of Elvis' records. Shaw was not impressed too much by the singing, but he realized that Elvis Presley could be a saleable commodity, so he agreed to take all Elvis' Sun singles to New York with him, and try to get them airplay.

The records were considered too 'country' for New York, but they were given plugs on a Cleveland Radio station by DJ Bill Randle, and he gained enough interest in the recordings to tempt most of the major New York labels out of the woodwork.

Back in Memphis in August of 1955 Sam Phillips released what was to become Elvis' final record for Sun. It came from the last recording session and featured *Mystery Train* backed with *I Forgot To Remember To Forget*. This record and the previous single both made the national country music charts, so Elvis was finally beginning to receive nationwide recognition.

Two months later in a suite at New York's Warwick Hotel, four men shook hands over newly signed contracts. 'That's gonna be the best deal you ever made,' Tom Parker addressed the small neat man at his side.

'I sure hope so Tom, that's a hell of a lot of money we've just signed away.' The speaker was Frank Folsom, RCA Victor's president. He and Steve Scholes, RCA's A&R, had just met with Parker and Sam Phillips and ironed out a contract for Elvis' recording services. It was agreed that RCA would pay Sam $35,000 for Elvis' contract, which still had a year to run, and the rights to all Elvis' released and unreleased recordings. Another $5,000 would go to Elvis on the completion of the signing. By today's standards $40,000 is peanuts, but in 1955 it was a totally unheard of amount for such a deal.

Parker began more and more to orchestrate Elvis' professional life, although Bob Neal was still officially his manager. The first thing Parker did after RCA had signed the contract was to buy Elvis out of his Louisiana Hayride agreement, which still had six months to run.

Elvis was dismayed. 'Colonel, I love doin' the show, and the folks have been awful nice to me.'

But Parker was adamant: 'Son, you're havin' to git back to Shreveport every Saturday night, no matter where you are; they're only paying you standard rate, and most of all you could be out playing big dates or TV shows on a Saturday — hell, that's the best night of the week.' Elvis knew that from a strict business viewpoint Parker was right, but he felt a great sense of loyalty to the Hayride staff. He confided one night to Vernon: 'Daddy, I know the Colonel is doin' what's best for me, but I sure feel bad about lettin' all those folks down in Shreveport.' Vernon Presley looked puzzled. 'But son, Mr. Parker knows what's best; and besides he's gonna make you a lotta money.' Vernon had been completely overawed by Tom Parker's confident manner and the promise of big bucks.

Within a few weeks of signing Elvis, RCA released the five singles previously released on Sun. As a result, for a short period, all five singles were available on two different labels.

Leaving the Memphis City Court after acquittal on assault charges (see page 27).

1. *Good Rockin' Tonight* was written by Roy Brown, a black performer, and recorded in 1949 by Wyonnie Harris, and was another example of Elvis going back to old blues songs for recording material.

2. Marion Keisker added a verse to this song, as Elvis had forgotten the original. Mack David, the composer agreed as long as Marion's name did not appear on the writing credits.

3. If that unwritten contract had been adhered to, then today Scotty and Bill Black's estate would be better off by well over a million dollars apiece! That was very likely one of the details that Col. Tom Parker 'overlooked' when he took over Elvis' management.

4. The tune was recorded again in 1938 by another blues singer, Joe Williams. Elvis' finished version became *Milk Cow Blues Boogie*.

Chapter Four

Having spent Christmas at home, as was his usual custom, Elvis was summoned to his first recording session for RCA Records on January 10, 1956. It was just two days after his twenty-first birthday, and he was feeling slightly nervous at having to go into the studios.

The RCA studio at 1525, McGavock Street in Nashville was actually owned by the Methodist Television, Radio and Film Commission. RCA rented the Commission's meager facilities. These amounted to two rooms, one an office, the other a studio and control room. Probably by chance rather than design, the room which served as the studio also contained the old church building's stairwell, from which the staircase had been removed, and it had been discovered that by placing a singer at the bottom of this space, the resulting sound was distorted by a natural echo chamber, a technique used to good effect on Elvis' early recordings.

Steve Scholes, who was in charge of the session, and Tom Parker introduced Elvis to the extra musicians who had been brought in for the recording. 'These guys are gonna help to beef up the sound a little,' Scholes explained as he introduced Chet Atkins, who was to play rhythm guitar, and Floyd Cramer, a brilliant country pianist. 'And these guys here are gonna sing along on some choruses and fills and things,' He indicated Ben and Brock Speers, and Gordon Stoker, three singers of gospel pedigree, well versed in harmony singing, and vocal arrangement. Elvis looked over towards Scotty, Bill, and D. J. and smiled to himself; at least the main men are here, he thought, gaining much comfort from their presence.

The first song due to be recorded was Ray Charles' *I Gotta Woman*[5] and immediately the session kicked off, it was obvious there were going to be problems. Elvis was leaping about as though he was on stage, bobbing and weaving, even sinking down onto one knee at one stage, and continually dropping 'off mike'.

Scholes' voice came through the control room intercom. 'Whoa, Elvis, hold it son, you're gonna have to stand still while you sing; I can't keep you on the dials back here!'

The number was tried again, this time with Elvis rooted to the spot, but immediately the raw energy and feeling that was Elvis disappeared. Elvis was depressed and after six takes there was no hiding the fact that the number was definitely lacking something.

'Mr. Scholes, I'm sorry. I don't feel right, please don't ask me to stand still, if I don't move I can't sing.'

Elvis was not kidding; it was the way he had cut tracks at Sam Phillips' studio, moving as he sang, at times almost leaping around the studio, letting the one microphone pick everything up. Maybe that was part of the secret of the 'Sun Sound', who knows?

However, Steve Scholes was having none of it. He asked the studio engineer to rig up another couple of mikes on either side of the singer so that, no matter which way Presley moved, he would remain 'on mike'.

The other immediate problem was Elvis' guitar work. He was used to playing his big Martin acoustic D28 very hard, and the rhythm sound he coaxed from his instrument was almost like a percussion noise at times[6]; very much an ingredient of that early sound. But it was giving Scholes problems; the guitar kept 'overspilling' onto the vocal mikes. It was Chet Atkins who came to the rescue, offering Elvis one of his own special guitar picks which he sometimes used for rhythm guitar. Made of felt, the pick made a much softer sound, so Elvis was able to play as hard as he liked without interfering too much with the quality of the finished recording. After all, Atkins was there now to fill in on rhythm guitar.

The following day, in another three hour session similar to the one before, Elvis and the musicians put down two more songs to add to the three already in the can; the five songs which came from that first RCA session were *I Gotta Woman (Sweetie)*, *Heartbreak Hotel*, *Money Honey*, *I'm Counting On You*, and *I Was The One*.

The change in sound and style, between these recordings and the Sun records was immediately apparent. Steve Scholes is quoted as saying that Elvis' style had evolved through a heavy schedule on the road. To an extent, this was true; Presley had lost the lightness in his voice and was beginning to discover his lower register. Other factors contributing to the development of the Presley sound were Floyd Cramer's piano playing, by far the most interesting instrument on *Heartbreak Hotel*, and the vocal backings which, with their 'doo-wops' and 'waa-waa's', were a key ingredient in the ballads (*I Was The One* and *I'm Counting On You*). On the road Elvis had always been a 'rockabilly singer', while the first sessions in RCA's studio were turning him into a 'pop' singer.

Some rock critics and commentators consider it a fashionable point of view to state that, after the first five records on the Sun label, Elvis Presley never again in his career did anything original. However, the fact remains that if Elvis had never recorded anything but those first five records, or had stuck to the same sound (and the same label) he would almost certainly never have progressed beyond the status of a little-known 'cult' singer, as has been the case with many of the most talented rockabilly artists. Certainly, most fans of the King would argue that in January 1956 Elvis still had many classics ahead of him.

Most performers have to progress if they

---

5. Elvis' finished version was renamed *I Gotta Sweetie* to appeal more to the teenage element.

6. Later, at Sun Records, Johnny Cash tried for a similar sound by stuffing paper between the strings of his guitar to compensate for having no drummer in the group.

ELVIS KING

are to survive; as part of that progression they become more sophisticated and more professional in their outlook, removing in the process the rough edges, both from their performances and their attitude towards the commercial realities of success in the music business. In Elvis' case, in losing the first rawness and the naïveté that characterized the days at Sun, he lost something that was vital and different forever; it was impossible to reproduce that early sound no matter how many talented sessionmen were added by RCA. Yet the new sound pioneered at RCA Nashville was to produce some brilliant recordings, even if they were well removed from the Southern style of rockabilly that had been Elvis' launchpad.

What is clear is that Elvis would not likely have taken off nationally without a change of sound and style. Rockabilly and country music (which is how Elvis had been categorized to date) were not the favorite sounds of New York or Los Angeles, and it was essential that, if Presley was going to crack the key markets of the Northern and coastal metropolitan areas, he was going to have to go through something of a metamorphosis.

Later that January of 1956, Elvis was back doing what he most enjoyed, singing in front of a live audience in San Antonio, Texas. But his first appearances under the auspices of Colonel Tom Parker were a sharp contrast with earlier gigs. Whereas before Presley featured on country music package shows supported by other known and proven country acts, now his support acts were jugglers, comedians, and any mediocre variety act that the Colonel could book. Elvis was not completely unaware of why he was working with such motley acts, but he still questioned the Colonel's motives.

'Colonel, why can't I have just one country singer in the show?' Elvis would inquire.

Parker always responded quickly. 'I'll tell ya why; do you remember when you were upstaging Marty Robbins and Webb Pierce a few months back?' Elvis opened his mouth to answer, but before he could, the Colonel went on: 'Well, I don't want no other act comin' on these shows an takin' the attention away from you. By the time the audience has sat through this bunch o' deadbeats, they gonna be so glad to see ya come on stage, they won't care whether ya sing or shit ya pants, son, they gonna love ya!'

As usual, the Parker school of showbiz philosophy paid dividends. That sultry night in Texas the kids in the audience were listlessly watching a comedian trying to make himself heard above the catcalls and chants for Elvis; the frantic comic was struggling vainly against the tide of youthful abuse. The vocal group who followed fared little better, relinquishing the stage after two numbers, mainly unheard. After an interval of about thirty minutes, which Parker put to use by selling 8 x 10 black and white glossy photographs of Elvis, the stage was set for the entry of the gladiator.

The atmosphere had been built up so much, they could have wheeled on a cardboard cutout of Elvis, and the place would still have erupted.

However, this night there was to be no cardboard cutout. The spotlight cut the darkness on the first notes of 'Waaall, since ma baby left me...' and the auditorium was in the grip of hysteria that was soon to become familiar throughout America and the world.

After *Heartbreak Hotel* Elvis kicked straight into *That's Alright Mama*. It was an amazing sight: Elvis dressed in green jacket, a couple of sizes too large, dark blue pants with a green stripe down the side, red socks, and white shoes, moving his legs in a way that made them seem formed in rubber. He grabbed the mike as though he was about to strangle it, bent it over backwards as he sang into it, then leapt back upright while emphasizing some part of the song. At times he would get right down and lie on the floor with the mike at the side of him, still singing.

He went straight from *That's Alright* into *Long Tall Sally*, a song that was currently a hit for yet another black R&B singer, Little Richard. At this point Elvis would slow things down by performing one of his ballads such as *I Was The One*. The decline in pace gave him the chance to explore the front row of the audience, which was by now reaching out in unison in a vain attempt to touch the sweating singer.

Then it was another rocker with *Baby, Let's Play House*, before Elvis came around to his current big ballad *I Want You, I Need You, I Love You*, a blues ballad which Elvis gave the full treatment of sensuous movements and facial expressions.

He bowed out with a tremendous version of Big Mama Thornton's *Hound Dog*, leaving

Leaving the sound stage during work on Loving You

himself and the audience breathless and feeling somewhat like a wrung out wash leather.

Many of today's well-known singers were amongst those early audiences, and have publicly stated that watching the early Elvis performances had a tremendous influence on their own careers. Mac Davis, who in later years was to write some of Elvis' big hits, was tremendously impressed by the young Elvis, and wrote a song about the experience in 1980 called *Hooked On Music*. Davis wrote: 'I heard a boy named Elvis Presley sing *That's Alright Mama* on the radio; I've been hooked on music from that moment on.' Later in the same song is the following lyric:

Well, I finally got some tickets to see Elvis live and hot.

My girlfriend almost jumped my bones going back to the parking lot,

I knew that it was not my great physique, good looks, and charm, that left that Texas teenybopper's nail prints in my arm.

Country music star, Bob Luman, famous for his 1960 recording of *Let's Think About Living*, probably spoke for many when he talked about seeing Elvis perform in Kilgore, Texas. 'Man, I didn't believe it. This cat came out in red pants and a green coat, and a pink shirt and socks, and he had this sneer on his face, and he stood behind the mike for five minutes, I'll bet, before he even made a move. Then he hit this guitar lick, and he broke two strings. Hell, I'd been playing ten years and I hadn't broken a TOTAL of two strings. So there he was, these two strings dangling, and he hadn't done anything except break the strings yet, and these high school girls were screaming and fainting and running up to the stage, and then he started to move his hips real slow like he had a thing going for his guitar. That was Elvis Presley when he was about nineteen, playing Kilgore, Texas. He made chills run up my back. Man, like when your hair starts grabbing you at your collar. For the next nine days, he played one nighters around Kilgore, and after school every day me and my girl would get in the car and go wherever he was playing that night. That was the last time I tried to sing like Lefty Frizzell or Webb Pierce!'

While Elvis was touring the South yet again, it was announced that he, through the William Morris Agency, had been signed for an appearance on the Tommy and Jimmy

Backstage with Ed Sullivan

Dorsey 'Stage Show' with an option on another five weeks, and that January 28 was to be his first ever TV appearance, just two weeks after his initial RCA recording session.

The Dorsey show was a half hour program, sponsored by Nestlés, which went out every Saturday night on CBS TV. Its main competition was the popular 'Perry Como Show'. The Dorseys were having problems maintaining an audience, and to be honest they were desperate for anything that might give them any headway in the ratings war.

The program's producer Jackie Philbin was shown a photograph of Elvis by the William Morris office, and he remarked that he 'looked like a guitar-playing Marlon Brando'. Philbin wasn't particularly impressed by Elvis as a singer on hearing his records, but then the producer didn't care a damn. As he said: 'If I only booked performers I liked, I'd have nothing but trumpet players on the show, but I feel that Elvis will appeal to the majority of people.'

On January 28, 1956 Elvis, Scotty, Bill and D. J. arrived in New York for the first of the Dorsey shows. It was a wet and windy day, and Elvis' name was billed in very small letters on the marquee outside the CBS building in New York's theatrical district. Life went on pretty much as normal in the metropolis; New York was not really interested in this hot new country singer from Tennessee.

'I sure hope the folks are gonna like us,' Elvis said to the Dorsey Brothers backstage. 'They're gonna love you,' was Tommy's reply — he had never even heard an Elvis Presley record, let alone seen him work!

The first song Elvis sang that night after his simple and straight introduction was Carl Perkins' *Blue Suede Shoes*, which was at that time lying at Number Two in the charts. Perkins had been signed by Sam Phillips in 1955, and along with Johnny Cash, had worked many shows on the road with Elvis. After Elvis' departure from Sun Records, Perkins was the artiste Phillips had envisaged taking over Elvis' top position. Unfortunately a bad car accident in March of '56 en route for an appearance on the highly rated 'Perry Como Show' put Perkins out of the picture. Anyway, Elvis had beaten him to the punch by singing the song on this particular night.

Perkins was not bitter about it, or if he was, he didn't show it. He said of the situation: 'Elvis had the looks on me. The girls were going for him for more reasons than music. Elvis was hitting them with sideburns, flashy clothes and no ring on that finger. I had three kids. There was no way of keeping him from being the man in that music, but I've never felt bitter, always felt lucky to be in the business.'

Elvis introduced his second song of the night thus: 'Thank you very much, ladies and gentlemen, and now a little song that I have on record, on RCA Victor entitled *Heartbreak Hotel*. What followed might have been the biggest disaster in Elvis' short career. Instead of the song being played with the arrangement as it was on the record, it was given a big band arrangement, with the Dorsey band blowing their brains out behind the singer. The solo break, usually taken by Scotty and a piano, was handed over to a trumpet player (remembering Jackie Philbin's earlier remarks), who proceeded to hit the highest notes he could register, and only succeeded in losing completely the timing of the song. In short, it was a calamity. But, miraculously, no one seemed to notice, or if they did, Elvis' furious movements kept then distracted.

Heartbreak Hotel was released the same week as the TV show, and obviously benefitted from Elvis' screen appearance. It made Billboard's Top 100 by February, and within a week had risen to Number Twenty-Eight. It was well on its way to Number One, and Elvis Presley was a national success!

On January 30, 1956 Elvis was back in the studio to lay down more tracks for RCA — at the RCA Studio, 24th East Street, New York, to be precise. The musicians were the usual Scotty, Bill and D. J. with the addition of Shorty Long on piano. There were no back-up vocalists on this particular session, which probably explains why no ballads were recorded.

'Lemme hear that first demo again please, Mr. Scholes.' Elvis had listened to half a dozen 'demo' records which had been brought to the session, and he had been impressed by a couple of them. They had already recorded *Blue Suede Shoes*, *My Baby Left Me*, and another Arthur Gunter song, *So Glad You're Mine*. The demo that Elvis listened to again had been recorded by one Otis Blackwell,

who was also the writer of the song. It was called *Don't Be Cruel*.

'Yeah, I really like that one, let's do it.'

At that point Tom Parker interjected: 'Well, let's save that one till we're in Nashville, Elvis, I think there may be a problem.'

'Well, let's do it now, Colonel, we don't need more than the guys we have here.'

'Yeah, I know. It's not that,' replied Parker. 'We have a small problem on the publishing side; it'd be better if you save it until later, Elvis.'

What Parker meant was, until they could contact Blackwell, and get him to agree to have the song published through Hill and Range (the company who published all Elvis' songs at the time) — and more important, to agree to Elvis getting half writing credit, and therefore half writing royalties. It was one of the Colonel's more imaginative money-making schemes. If a songwriter wanted Elvis to record a new song and turn it into a hit he would have to agree to the Colonel's scheme. Otherwise, his boy would pass, it was as simple as that. Surprisingly, or perhaps not surprisingly, the writers usually agreed. Fifty percent of a smash hit was better than a hundred percent of nothing.

This particular recording session stretched over three days, through Tuesday 31st, and was finished off on the following Friday, February 3. In addition to the three songs already mentioned they also cut *Lawdy Miss Clawdy*, a hit in 1952 for its author Lloyd Price; *One Sided Love Affair*; Little Richard's self-penned hit *Tutti Frutti*; *I'm Gonna Sit Right Down And Cry Over You*, which had been recorded earlier by R&B artiste Roy Hamilton; and *Shake, Rattle and Roll*, yet another song with a black origin, this time as a 1954 recording by Big Joe Turner.

February 4, 1956 found Elvis, Scotty, Bill, and D. J. back in the CBS TV studios in New York, for their second appearance on the Dorsey show. Although the Dorseys and their backers had come in for some flak from the critics, and certain sections of the public, the mail for the program had doubled following Elvis' first appearance, so he was promptly signed up for another five appearances, to follow on consecutive Saturdays.

On this second show, Elvis performed *Tutti Frutti* (with a particularly expressive dance on the balls of his feet during Scotty's guitar solo, which brought shouts of delight and applause from the studio audience) and the ballad *I Was The One*. Audience appreciation was noticeably better than the previous week, and Elvis looked pleased.

Elvis sat in the wings of the stage after the show, a towel wrapped around his head prizefighter style, his head tipped back as if he were searching for air. His fingers continually drummed on his knees, and his feet tapped out a rhythm. His incredible nervous energy was taking over; he rose and paced the corridor a couple of times, before walking out onto the now near deserted sound stage, and sitting behind D. J. Fontana's drums. There for another half hour, he sat and drummed and tapped and fiddled until he had played out his tensions. Only then did he return to the dressing room and change into his street clothes.

The next six days were taken up by one-night stands. The pace was hard; a long drive between shows, check in at a hotel, clean up, do the show, back to the hotel to sleep, and up the following morning to begin the whole routine over. The next Saturday, February 11, it was back to New York for the Dorsey show. On this, his third TV appearance, Elvis was introduced by Bill Randle, one of New York's biggest DJs, and the man who first played Elvis' records on radio around the New York area.

His introduction ran: 'We'd like at this time to introduce you to a young fella, who like many performers, Johnny Ray among them, came up out of nowhere to be overnight very big stars.'

In the wings Elvis held back a snarl of contempt at this remark. 'Shit! what does he think we do when we're not on TV, wait around and do nothin'? Where's he get this "out of nowhere" crap from?'

Randle continued: 'This young fella we saw for the first time making a movie short, and we think tonight he's gonna make television history for ya, we'd like you to meet him now — Elvis Presley!'

Elvis performed *Shake, Rattle And Roll* ending the song with a snatch of *Flip, Flop And Fly*, and in the second half he did *I Gotta Woman*.

At this point in his career Elvis was having to fly to some of his engagements. He didn't like it, but it was necessary. He employed Bobby 'Red' West, an old school friend, to drive all the instruments and spare clothes to

E L V I S

50

K I N G

wherever they were appearing on the Sunday, then immediately after the Dorsey shows, Elvis, Scotty, Bill, and D. J. would fly to the engagement. But for this routine, it would have become impossible by now to keep up the schedule of live performances as well as the TV shows.

February 18, 1956 was the date for Elvis' fourth Dorsey appearance. He performed a superb version of *Baby, Let's Play House* which really rocked, with Scotty Moore particularly outstanding on guitar. It was noticeable that after that first disastrous attempt at accompanying Elvis, the Dorsey band took no part in these performances. The second number was *Tutti Frutti*, which Elvis introduced as 'A little song that really tells a story, it makes a lot of sense!' — then he bawled out the first line: 'A wop bop a loo bop, alop bam boom!'

For Elvis' fifth and penultimate appearance on the Dorsey program, he sang *Blue Suede Shoes* — which Elvis described as 'his latest RCA escape — I mean release!' — and *Heartbreak Hotel* which this time was performed without the 'help' of the Dorsey Orchestra, apart from the last two bars.

March 24, 1956, a bitter day, with snow filling the Manhattan sky, marked the King's last appearance on the Dorsey show. By this time the producers were finding no problems selling the tickets. In fact there weren't enough to go round, and the CBS TV Theatre audience was noticeably younger than it had been just two months earlier at the start of Elvis' six appearances.

Jimmy Dorsey introduced Elvis again with the words: 'Here he is — Elvis Presley!' — by now the big build up had become redundant. Elvis struck a chord on his guitar, leant into the microphone and sang; 'You know the landlord rang my front door bell....' and the next few bars of *Money Honey* were lost amidst screams and yells. His second number was again *Heartbreak Hotel* because, he said, 'they had received a lot of mail since last week wanting to hear it again.'

The pressure of work was by now became immense, and gradually the traveling got to Elvis. That spring he collapsed and was taken to hospital in Jacksonville, Florida. He was ordered to rest for at least a week, but discharged himself the day after his admission to carry on with the tour.

Heartbreak Hotel had made Number One in the Billboard charts, stayed on top for seven weeks, and remained in the charts for a total of 27 weeks. It also made Number One in the country music chart, and spent 27 weeks in those charts as well. It entered the R&B charts, peaking at Number Five and staying in the charts for thirteen weeks.

On the last day of March, Elvis' first album, called simply *Elvis Presley* entered the Billboard L P charts. It spent 49 weeks in the chart, including a spell at the top. The album contained a dozen songs; *Blue Suede Shoes, I Gotta Woman (Sweetie), Tutti Frutti, Money Honey, I'm Counting On You, One Sided Love Affair, I'm Gonna Sit Right Down And Cry Over You* plus five songs which had been inherited from Sun Records when RCA gained Elvis' signature. They were *Trying To Get To You, I Love You Because, Blue Moon, I'll Never Let You Go (Little Darlin')* and *Just Because*. The album had a monochrome photograph of Elvis on the front looking very young, his mouth open in a pained expression of raw feeling, strumming wildly on his guitar. Down the left hand side of the cover was printed in large pink letters the word Elvis, and across the bottom of the cover was Presley in equal-sized green letters.

It was becoming obvious that no matter what critics were writing or saying, Elvis was destined to become a hot property, and Hollywood, always on the lookout for any new trend on which money could be made, showed interest in the new boy.

April 1, 1956 found Elvis at Paramount Film Studios in California. Tom Parker was deep in conversation with Hal Wallis, the film producer who had arranged a film test for the young rock 'n' roll singer. Wallis' most recent discoveries had been Dean Martin and Jerry Lewis, with whom he was enjoying great success, and he saw Elvis as the new James Dean. He made it plain to Parker that he was interested in sex appeal rather than acting ability.

Elvis was waiting for his call, talking with his cousin Gene Smith. 'I think this is gonna be my big break, Gene; if I can become a movie star, I can go on for ever. Singing ain't gonna last more'n two or three years, singers come and go, but good actors last a long time.' It was obvious he was delighted, and he could hardly hide his excitement at getting this chance. Wallis had arranged for one of his veteran actors, Frank Faylen, to act with Elvis in the test, and they went through part of a script from a Wallis film currently under production. Elvis was given parts of the script which conveyed a wide range of emotions, and he ran through them competently after a slow start.

Faylen encouraged Elvis to be a little tougher in the more emotional scenes, realising that the young man had never acted in his life and was underplaying the scenes.

Hal Wallis was impressed enough to state: 'I felt the same thrill I experienced when I first saw Errol Flynn on the screen; Elvis, in a very different modern way, had exactly the same power, virility, and sexual drive.' He was impressed enough by Elvis' acting and Tom Parker's bargaining to offer a seven year, three film contract worth $100,000 for the first movie, $150,000 for the second, and $200,000 for the third one.

On April 3, 1956 Elvis made an appearance on the 'Milton Berle Show', which was broadcast from an aircraft carrier moored at San Diego, California. The show was watched by an estimated TV audience of forty million people. On the show Elvis performed *Heartbreak Hotel*, *Money Honey*, and *Blue Suede Shoes*.

Things were going great. Too well, in fact. Elvis' burgeoning career was coming ever more under the sway of the showman and self-styled 'Colonel' Tom. And why not? As spring headed into summer it seemed difficult to put a foot wrong. Thanks to those TV appearances, Elvis had become big business and Parker's biggest headache seemed to be asking for the right money at a time when his boy's stock was rising almost faster than anyone could keep count. But just as the world appeared to be Presley's oyster, when finding somewhere to play was the least of anybody's problems, the Colonel made a mistake which was to hound Elvis for the next thirteen years.

Parker booked Elvis into the Frontier Hotel in Las Vegas for two weeks, at a reported $8,500 a week. It may have seemed like a good idea at the time, but the Las Vegas audiences were certainly not Elvis' scene. In '56, the gambling city's audiences were very much middle-aged and upwards, very conservative in their outlook. It was a far cry from the adoring young females and their escorts which normally made up an

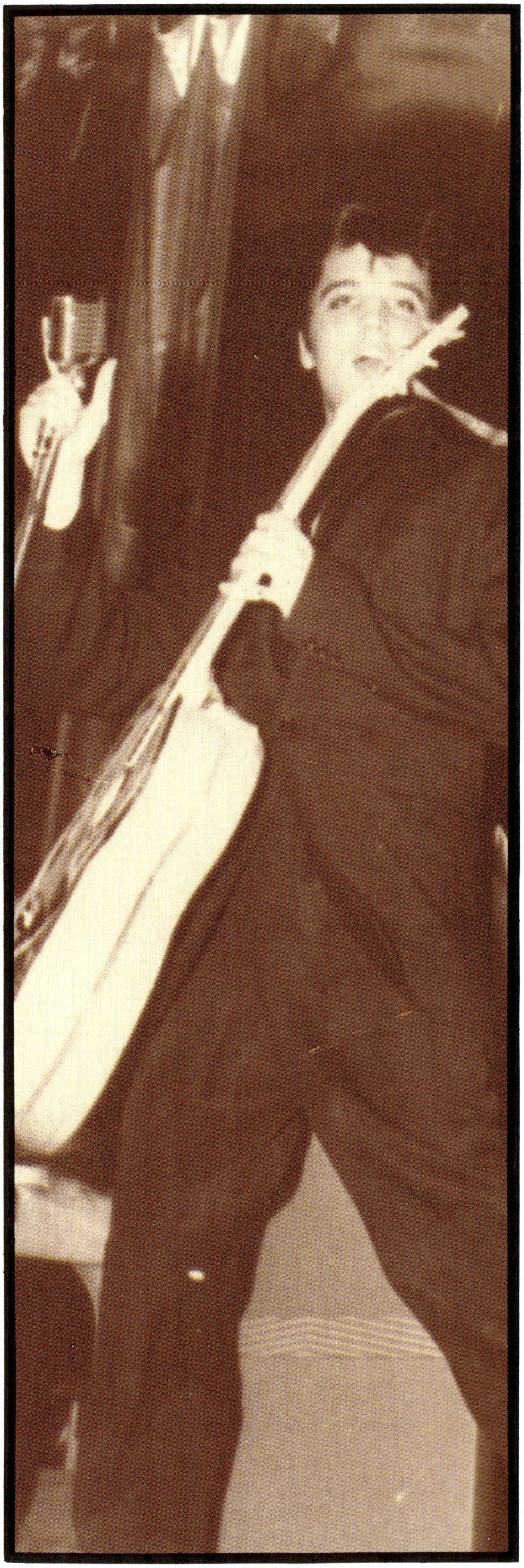

Elvis Presley audience.

Elvis started his run at the Hotel on April 23 in the Venus Room. The billing outside the hotel read: 'Freddie Martin and his Band — Sheckey Greene — and special added attraction, Elvis Presley.' (Greene was a comedian of the time.) To say that the audiences hated him would be a little harsh, but they were definitely ice-cool.

Most of the punters, it must be said, were there out of curiosity, to see the strange young man who had caused a sensation on TV. Not out of adulation.

The people shuffled in their seats and applauded politely, but they most definitely did NOT scream and shout, and for the first time in a still developing career since the ill-fated appearance on the Grand Ole Opry, Elvis was playing to a totally silent audience. His music didn't suffer, he sang as enthusiastically as ever, with Scotty, Bill and D. J. doing sterling work at the back, but the audience remained unmoved, stunned by a combination of amazement, aloofness and complete indifference.

It has been widely, but falsely, recorded that Elvis didn't complete the full two weeks engagement. He did, under great duress, complete the engagement, but by closing night Elvis' obvious dislike for the venue and Las Vegas audiences was given free rein in his sarcasm.

For the final show Presley was waiting nervously in the wings, remarking to one of the back stage staff how glad he would be to get back on the road in front of his own fans, and away from Vegas. The compere was already on stage, announcing Elvis. 'Everywhere he went, he was breaking records, and speaking of records, he is the Number One selling record artiste in the country, RCA's pride and joy, and this is his last performance, we regretfully have to say tonight, we hate to see him go, he's a fine young lad, and a fine talent — let's welcome, ladies and gentlemen, Elvis Presley.'

Subdued applause brought Elvis out of the wings to the centre of the stage with that familiar awkward walk, guitar slung around his neck. On reaching the mike, he struck a chord on the guitar, and wailed the opening bars of *Heartbreak Hotel*.

A real Presley audience would have met the opening of this particular song with screams which drowned out the following bars. Here in Vegas, it was met with stony silence. Elvis shot a glance at Bill Black, completely unnerved at the prospect of having to go through the song with no reaction at all; sweat started trickling down his forehead, but it was the product of nerves bordering on terror, not effort or exhaustion.

After the desultory approval which greeted the end of the song, an obviously dispirited Elvis muttered: 'Thank you very much, ladies and gentlemen, we'd like to say it's been a sorta pleasure being in Las Vegas. This makes our second week here, and tonight's our last night, and we've had a pretty hard time...ah — had a pretty good time while we were here! Now we've got a few little songs we'd like to do for ya, we have on record, in our style of singin'.. if you wanna call it singin'... and here's one that I hope ya like, and this song really tells a story friends, it's not only sad, it's plumb pitiful! — plumb pitiful!' This raised a few titters from the soporific audience. 'It's called *Long Tall Sally* and I want you to listen to this song, it really tells a story.'

Again Elvis gave the delivery of the song everything, but once more it was met by barely polite applause. 'Thank you,' Elvis said as he finished the song, his lips curling in a gesture of savage sarcasm, 'music lovers!' Scotty and Bill smiled at each other as Elvis turned round with a 'that told 'em' look on his face.

'Thank you friends, here's one more little song we'd like to do for ya, to do this song we'd like to call on Mr. Freddie Martin and wonderful orchestra to back us up, back us completely up!

'Night before last on the stage of this here audito....ah — this place here, RCA Victor awarded me a gold record for the millionth sale of *Heartburn Motel* which we did a little earlier out here, and we're real proud of it because it made so much mon... ah — it's done so well for itself, and here's another one comin' right up behind it, we hope will hit the million mark, it's called Get outta the stables grandmaw, you're too old to be horsin' around.

At this the audience began to stir. This was a Las Vegas kind of joke.

Elvis sensed the mood and pressed on with his theme: 'This song's called the *Blue Suede Shoes*. Then turning to Freddie Martin he

Left: **Mean and moody.**

Above and p.58: Hollywood soon tried to smooth the rough edges off Elvis by posing him with starlets for the gossip pages. Here with the "World's Most Photogenic Girl"; overleaf with Barbara Long, Elvis' *Loving You* co-star.

remarked: 'Do you know that song, Mr. Martin, Get outta the stables? — Ya do? Well, do you know that one about 'take back your golden garter my leg is turning green' d'ya ever hear that one? — well, let's do *Blue Suede* — ah sumpin'.'

Before he got into the song Elvis dedicated it to two stars who were in the audience, Ray Bolger the fifties film star, and Phil Silvers the very popular comedian of that time.

Elvis' preamble to the song seemed to have warmed the audience a little, and when he left the stage at the end of the song he received an enthusiastic round of applause. The compere brought Elvis back on for an encore to which he replied: 'Thank you, friends, I was comin' back on anyway! — no sincerely I'm just about too pooped to pop, ah friends we gotta song here we got on record, this song has really been a big seller for me — it sold 43!... the song is called *Money Honey*.'

If the Frontier Hotel was a calamity, everything else in Elvis' life was rosy, and with the money he was earning he bought a new house. He already owned three Cadillacs, so the next step was a better, bigger house. It was situated at 1034, Audubon Drive in Memphis' Audubon Park area, and cost him $40,000. The house was a single storey building, consisting of three bedrooms, a living room, a games room, dining room, and sitting room. When he moved in, Elvis had a swimming pool built at the back of the house. If Elvis and his parents were supremely happy, the other residents of Audubon Drive soon became less than ecstatic about their near neighbors. The biggest problem was the fans; day and night they trampled gardens and flower beds, peered through windows, stripped lawns, and even scraped dust off Elvis' bright new Caddies.

But another barrier was snobbery. The residents didn't want this young tearaway and his poor white trash family living in the neighborhood. Malicious gossip began to spread. 'That Presley woman, she hangs her washing out on the line! My dear, how common can one get?' Things got so Elvis had to have a stone wall topped with metal spikes built around the house, both to segregate it from the gentile folk of Audubon Drive and to try to keep out the fans. But stone walls and metal spikes didn't cause Presley fans too much trouble.

Fan fever had begun to run so high by now, that Elvis had to pay dearly for any privacy. At evenings he might hire the local amusement park or the fairground. He'd pay the owner to open up at night when there was no one else around, and he and his friends would enjoy themselves untroubled by screaming fans. Whenever Elvis dated a girl, it was more often than not to the amusement park that he would take her.

On the 5 June, 1956 Elvis made his second appearance on television's 'Milton Berle Show', an appearance which was to attract some of the severest criticism of his career. Elvis came on and opened with *Hound Dog*, to squeals of sheer delight from the audience — he was back on familiar territory. Elvis gave the song a particularly torrid ending, slowing down the song to a blues style, and wriggling in his most expressive fashion. It was those antics which prompted the criticism.

At the end of the song, Milton Berle came on amidst the squeals and screams which were Elvis', and proceeded to mimic the young singer's actions to the tune of *Hound Dog*. He really made a meal of it, and then as if to rectify his antics, Berle thundered, 'How about my boy, how 'bout him, huh?'

Berle was an old ham, and he was hogging the limelight.

At rehearsals for the show, Elvis had problems staying on the chalk lines put down for camera positions. Berle had said to him, 'You or me, one of us is gonna be outta camera, and it's not gonna be me!' He came across strong in his patter with Elvis. 'I don't know what you're screaming at... the way these girls are flipping their lids down here... I'm gonna tell ya, that beat with your foot is absolutely sensational, I wanna ask you somethin' Elvis, if I did that thing the same way you did it, do you think I could get all the girls the same way you do?'

'Well, it might not help you to get girls,' Elvis replied, 'but at your age it sure helps to keep blood circulating!'

Berle couldn't resist getting one back, 'You make me sound like a used car,' he replied. 'My tail light may be dragging, but my battery is still charging!'

This brought a round of applause from the studio audience. Milton Berle 1, Elvis Presley 0, that showed 'em that the old troopers can't be upstaged by these young upstarts. Berle was the STAR of this show, and he wanted it

ELVIS

KING

to be obvious.

'Elvis, what do you do with your hair, is it Toni you use?' Berle continued. 'I wanna tella ya, how can I get these girls to scream over me this way, I really mean that?'

'Mr. Berle, I don't think you'd like it, I don't like it, all these girls tryin' to rip your clothes off, tryin' to kiss ya and everything.'

Berle made a great play of feigning surprise. 'You don't?' Then as an aside to the audience: 'Somebody musta stamped on his head with those *Blue Suede Shoes*!'

Elvis replied that he would prefer a quieter type of girl, somebody who would calm him down and relax him, 'I tell you Mr. Berle the kinda girl I like would be somebody like Debra Paget.' Of course it was a set up. Berle told Elvis that Deborah Paget was not in his league, and to 'stick with *Heartbreak Hotel*, and stay away from the Waldorf.' She wouldn't even notice him. Then they brought Miss Paget on, and she proceeded to go wild and scream when introduced to Elvis.

Most of Milton Berle's introductions for Elvis were excuses for him to introduce gags into the proceedings, and after another hammy interlude Elvis sang *I Want You, I Need You, I Love You*.

Berle came back to center stage after this song in a more serious mood. 'Ladies and gentlemen, I don't think I'm revealing any secrets when I tell you that Elvis Presley is the fastest rising young singer in the entertainment industry today, and as proof of this, Elvis, I would like to present this to you. It's a great award from one of the great theatrical periodicals of all time, it's the 'Billboard', they present you this. I'd like to read it for you: 'This triple crown award presented to Elvis Presley for his RCA Victor recording *Heartbreak Hotel*.

The show was certainly a success, and probably the most satisfying TV show that Elvis had done to date; however, the critics lashed it. Jack Gould, TV critic for the New York Times said:

'Mr. Presley has no discernible singing ability. His speciality is rhythm songs which he renders in an undistinguished whine; his phrasing, if it can be called that, consists of stereotyped variations that go with a beginner's aria in a bath tub. For the ear he is an unutterable bore, not nearly so talented as Frank Sinatra back in the latter's rather hysterical days at the Paramount Theatre. Nor does he convey the emotional fury of a Johnny Ray.

'From watching Mr. Presley it is wholly evident that his skill lies in other directions. He is a rock 'n' roll variation of one of the most standard acts in show business: the virtuoso of the hootchy-kootchy. His one speciality is an accented movement of the body that heretofore has been primarily identified with the repertoire of the blond bombshells of the burlesque runway. The gyration never had anything to do with the world of popular music and still doesn't.'

Sunday morning, July 1, 1956. Elvis and his musicians and entourage are waking up on the overnight sleeper train as it pulls into Pennsylvania station. All the guys are sleepy still, after a hard show the night before in Richmond, Virginia. Elvis is reading fan mail, and D. J. Fontana is making remarks about the girls in the photographs which seem to be in every letter that Elvis opens. 'I sure don't know where all the letters come from,' Elvis remarks, looking genuinely puzzled. 'I didn't know there were this many girls in the world.'

'There sure are,' replies D. J. 'and I think they were all in that theatre last night!' Elvis laughs at the recollection; it certainly had been a hot steamy night in Richmond.

Elvis was in New York for yet another appearance on TV, this time on the newly instated 'Steve Allen Show' which had been designed to compete with the highly popular, and highly rated 'Ed Sullivan Show' on the rival CBS channel. Steve Allen had been told to sign big names, and he had obliged with people like Steve Lawrence and Eydie Gorme, Sammy Davis Jr. and The Will Mastin Trio, and film star Kim Novak. It was obvious that in the popular music world, particularly the young end of it, the name to have on the show was Elvis Presley.

Elvis and his musicians arrived outside the Hudson Theater in two taxis. Elvis had been interested in the New York Sunday Mirror on the way from the station, the headline had caught his eye: '2 airliners missing — 127 aboard' recalled his own fear of flying; in particular, it chillingly recalled the near accident that Elvis and the boys had encountered back in April flying to Nashville for a recording session. Their chartered plane had almost collided with another air-

After the pre-induction medical

craft over Texas. The incident had shaken Presley so badly that he only recorded one song at the session before going home to Memphis to recover.

The Hudson Theater had been converted into a television studio. The stage had been enlarged to accommodate the cameras, and the balcony had been taken over by the lights and the producer's control room. That left only about a dozen rows of seats for the live audience.

Inside the theatre, in his dressing room,

ELVIS

Elvis ran the ever present comb through his greased hair, adjusted his grey silk suit, and removed what dirty marks he could from his white buck shoes. In fact the outfit was the same as he'd worn the night before; the frenetic pace of the band's schedule of one-night stands didn't leave much time for fresh clothes. There was a knock on the door, and a short, bald man asked 'Mr. Presley?'

'You can call me Elvis.'

'Okay,' the guy replied. 'Elvis, Mr. Allen would like to see everyone in the orchestra area in about ten minutes.'

At the rehearsal, Elvis ran through what was to be his first number on the show, *I Want You, I Need You, I Love You*, without moving at all. He just stood, guitar hanging around his neck, and sang.

He rehearsed his other song, *Hound Dog*, with a full grown bassett hound which was sat on a podium in front of Elvis looking sorrowful. Try as he might, Elvis couldn't get the pooch to look at him while he was singing. The director was happy enough though, and after rehearsing a comedy sketch in which he was due to feature, Elvis retired to his dressing room.

A gaggle of newsmen and columnists waited for him. This was Elvis' first appearance in New York since the Dorsey shows and with the amount of criticism that had flown under the bridge since then, the press were keen for Presley's reaction to some of the rougher receptions he'd been receiving of late. He sat at one end of his dressing room flanked by Colonel Parker and the Colonel's right hand man, Tom Diskin.

Elvis was amazingly cool and charming, in sharp contrast to what the reporters had been expecting. He answered all their questions the best he could.

'What do you think about the criticism you've been getting? Do you get mad when they call you Elvis the Pelvis?'

'Well, I think that's a pretty dumb comment. I can't tell reporters what to say, you know, they have a job that they have to do, and I can just do what I think is right.'

'Are you nervous about your performance tonight in front of a national audience?'

'No, sir, I think I'm prepared.'

'What do you think about the skit?'

'I think it's pretty funny.'

'Have you ever worked with Imogene Coca and Andy Griffith before?'

'No sir, but I'm looking forward to it. They're some of my favorite performers.'

'Elvis, are you going out with any one girl right at this moment?'

'No, sir, I have occasional dates, but I'm not going with any one girl right now.'

'Thank you, ladies and gentlemen,' Tom Parker finally interjected. 'I'm afraid that's gotta be the last question right now, we have a dress rehearsal comin' up soon.'

When the reporters had gone, Elvis turned to Parker and said: 'Colonel, you know not one of those folks asked me about my music, not one.'

Parker was more interested in other things. 'Elvis, Mr. Allen has asked me to tell you that he don't want you to move whilst you're doin' the songs tonight.'

Elvis opened his mouth to object. 'Well, I know, son,' Parker went on. 'I know that it ain't you, but the folks here, Mr. Allen 'n all, they think that you been gettin' too much bad publicity from the other shows you done, and they wanna try things, well, a little different.'

'A little different' wasn't the half of it. When it came to Elvis' part of the show at the actual broadcast, Steve Allen announced him reading from the 'idiot cards': 'Well, you know, a couple of weeks ago on The Milton Berle Show, our next guest, Elvis Presley, received a great deal of attention which some people seemed to interpret one way, and some viewers interpreted another. Naturally, it's our intention to do nothing but a good show. We want to do a show the whole family can watch and enjoy, and we always do, and, tonight, we're presenting Elvis Presley in his — ha, ha, — what you might call his first comeback.' This brought chuckles from the audience. '...And at this time it gives me extreme pleasure to introduce the new Elvis Presley. Here he is.'

Elvis wandered out into the spotlight, holding his guitar by the neck at his side, but he was not dressed in the usual jacket, pants and shirt, but in a set of tails, with a powder blue shirt with matching bow tie! The audience didn't quite know whether to applaud or just stare. There were in fact a few sniggers. Allen greeted Elvis' entrance with: 'Elvis, I must say you look absolutely wonderful, you really do, and I think your millions of fans are really going to get a kick seeing a different side of your personality tonight.'

ELVIS

'Thank you, Mr. Allen, uh....it's not too often I get to wear the uh.. suit 'n tails, and all this stuff, but I think I have on something tonight which is not quite correct for evening wear.'

'Not quite formal, what's that Elvis?'

'*Blue Suede Shoes!*'

The audience roared as Elvis indicated that he was in fact wearing a pair of blue suede shoes.

'Well, Elvis you've certainly been a real good sport about the whole thing, and now I have a little surprise for you. Gene, could I have the surprise.' Allen was handed a large roll of paper. The audience and Elvis waited. Was this another play for a cheap laugh at Presley's expense? Mercifully not. Allen went on: 'This, Elvis, believe it or not, is a giant petition that was signed by three giants out in the alley.' This again drew slightly strained laughter from the audience. 'No seriously, this was signed by over eighteen thousand of Elvis' loyal fans saying they wanted to see him soon again on television. It was sent to us the other day by our good friend DJ Don Wallace, in Tulsa, Oklahoma. Eighteen thousand signatures on this, Elvis it's a fine thing.'

Elvis thanked Allen in his usual hesitant, humble manner, and Allen then asked Elvis what he was going to sing that night. *I Want You, I Need You, I Love You*, replied Elvis, which was greeted by applause from the audience. The curtains opened to reveal Scotty, Bill, and D. J. sat within a stage set which resembled an old Roman temple, and coupled with Elvis in bow tie and tails, this certainly presented a unique vision of the King in action.

At the end of the song, Allen returned on stage. Making patronizing noises, he took Elvis' guitar, and left the stage to just Elvis and a bassett hound sitting on a small podium just below head height in front of Elvis. Besides a wonderfully doleful expression, the dog was wearing a bow tie and a top hat. The audience was amused. Elvis grabbed the mike stand, leaned forward, looked the dog straight in the eye, and chanted: 'You Ain't Nuthin' But A Hound Dog'. The dog was unimpressed.

Presley worked his way through the song; he moved back and forth in his tracks, he crouched down, he circled the animal — she was totally unmoved. At the end of the number, Elvis smiled, planted a kiss on the dog, and walked off stage to great applause.

Elvis' next portion of the show was a take off of the 'Grand Ole Opry', in which he was joined by Allen, Imogene Coca, and Andy Griffith. A mock barnyard was set up, and each of the principals was dressed like a dimestore cowboy, with Elvis in black shirt, red bandana, black cowboy hat, and sporting a six shooter and holster.

Allen proceeded to introduce each person comically. When he reached Elvis, who for the purpose of the sketch was called 'Tumbleweed', he said: 'I'll tell you about this fella. He is a trick rider. You ain't seen trick riding until you've seen Tumbleweed.

'Yesterday he went across the range on a full gallop blindfolded, and he picked up a rattlesnake with his teeth; he jumped four fences and he dropped that snake into a gopher hole at a full galop. Tell 'em why it was so tough, Tumbleweed?"

With a straight face Elvis replied; 'I don't use no horse.' There then followed a cod commercial for a fictitious candy bar called 'Tonto', which ended with Elvis shooting the candy bar as it jumped from Allen's hands.

The sketch ended with a 'country' song on which each performer took a verse. When it was Elvis' turn he bellowed:

    Well I gotta horse and I gotta gun
    And I'm going out and have some fun
    I'm a-warning you galoots
    Don't step on my blue suede boots.

It was pure corn, but a perfect example of fifties television presentation, where guests not only did their own 'thing', but joined in sketches and skits with the shows' stars. However, even this early in his career, Elvis' fans did not relish seeing him in this kind of cornball situation; they wanted to see him in action, singing in his own inimitable style.

Allen came in for a great deal of criticism from the growing army of Presley fans for what he put Elvis through on the TV show, although most of the critics were apparently in favor of it. Jack O'Brien of the New York Herald wrote: 'Elvis Presley was a cowed kid on Steve Allen's opus last night... NBC's promise to de-gyrate the controversial hip-swinging singer was kept...It proved Presley's excitement is not his voice, but his erotic presentation...Best 'guests' on the show were Steve Lawrence and Eydie Gorme...As for the pelvis, once his gears were shifted into a picture suitable for a Sunday evening, it was plain he couldn't sing or act a lick...'

It was a similar story from Jack Gould in the New York Times: 'Elvis Presley was a most sedate individual last night...his distasteful gyrations were eliminated, in so far as this corner is concerned the young man has lost none of his indescribable monotony as a singer...if Mr. Presley behaves himself in other respects, he now is certainly entitled to pursue his career on TV.'

Monday, July 2, 1956, and RCA's New York studios on East 24th Street were again playing host to the hottest new singer in the U.S. of A., who had commandeered Number 1 studio to cut some new tracks.

After the cramped studios of Sun Records, RCA's Number 1 was unashamed luxury to Elvis and the boys. It was a large rectangular room lined with acoustic tiles, and sound deadening half cylinder-shaped protuberances on the walls. In the middle of the studio was a rectangular-shaped piece of carpet on which the musicians had set up their instruments. Scotty was on electric guitar, Bill on double bass, D. J. on drums, and Shorty Long on piano. The Jordanaires were also on hand for background vocal duties.

Steve Scholes, shirt sleeves rolled up, strolled into the studio and suggested to Elvis that the band record *Hound Dog*. 'I don't know, Mr. Scholes, I'm not so sure about recording it, I only do it in the stage shows as a kinda fill in.'

'Yeah, but it sure as hell goes down well,' was Scholes' reply. 'I'm convinced you should cut it Elvis, especially after last night.'

At the mention of the show the previous night, Elvis fell about laughing. 'Man, that was a joke! Ain't nobody gonna buy no record after seeing that performance.' Presley was sick about the way he'd been presented on the Steve Allen show.

'Well, I think you'll do well with it,' argued Scholes. 'It sure goes well on your live dates.'

Finally Scholes persuaded Elvis to give the song a try.

Seventeen takes later, and Elvis was not a happy man. Stood over in the corner by the playback speaker, leaning on the wall, his head bowed in concentration, he was listening to playback Number Eighteen. But Presley just wasn't satisfied: 'Let's try it again, Mr. Scholes.'

After thirty takes the group figured that

they likely had a good take in the can somewhere. Scotty groaned: 'Man, if I play that lick one more time, I'll go outta my mind.' They had a break for lunch, which consisted of sandwiches brought in from outside by Elvis' cousin Junior Smith, and Coke, and as they ate Elvis listened to all the best playbacks from thirty takes of *Hound Dog*. He sat crosslegged in front of the speaker listening intently. Everybody threw in suggestions, but the final decision lay with Elvis, and he decided with a big grin that take twenty-eight was the one.

After lunch Steve Scholes brought in another pile of demos for Elvis to listen to. Elvis picked out three titles, and handed them to the engineer to play. The first one was *Anyway You Want Me*, a ballad which Elvis seemed to like, and one of the others was the same song which he had picked out at the earlier New York session, Otis Blackwell's *Don't Be Cruel*.

The Colonel had cleared up the publishing 'technicalities' with Blackwell, and the song was now available for Elvis to record. 'I wanna try this one, Mr. Scholes; it's a great song, there's somethin' about it I like.' Leaning with one hand on the wall, holding the sheet music in the other, Elvis listened intently to the demo of *Don't Be Cruel* once more. As it finished he turned to Scholes and announced: 'That's the one I want to try.'

After a quick solo run-through of the song, during which Elvis accompanied himself on guitar, he made some changes to the rhythm pattern which Shorty noted down on the sheet music. The Jordanaires chipped in with their ideas for the vocal backings, and Scotty worked out an intro on the electric guitar. The whole thing took only twenty minutes to arrange, after which Elvis asked: 'Whaddya think, Mr. Scholes?'

Scholes suggested they try it. Eight takes later it was done, and one of Elvis' classic recordings was captured for ever on tape. Though no one present in the studio at that time saw it coming, *Hound Dog* coupled with *Don't Be Cruel* was to sell five million copies within a year, making it one of Elvis' biggest successes of the fifties.

On Independence Day, 1956 Elvis arrives home for the first time in months. Home is still 1034, Audubon Drive, Memphis, and it is at the city's Russwood Stadium that Elvis will perform that night. The train from New York had deposited Elvis and his entourage that afternoon at Memphis station, and Elvis is taking the opportunity to spend a few hours with his parents and family.

Elvis is playing the records he had made in New York; Steve Scholes has made some quick pressings overnight for Elvis' approval which he had brought home with him. Elvis' paternal grandmother, Minnie Presley, is sitting on the couch listening intently; his mother bobs her head in now and then from the kitchen; sitting next to Elvis is a female companion by the name of Barbara.

'How do you like it?' Elvis throws out the question to no one in particular, and it is Barbara who answers. 'I think it's very good, and I like it.'

'Do you want to hear the other song?' This time Minnie Presley nods. Elvis puts *Anyway You Want Me* on the turntable, to the approval of his grandmother and his mother.

'Are you going to sing that song tonight?' Gladys asks.

'I don't think so, Ma; we've only just learned it.'

The early evening is a madhouse of rabid activity in the Presley household, as everyone gets ready to go to the show. It is to be a real family outing; the entire Presley clan is proud of its boy's homecoming after his achievements on nationwide TV.

Russwood Stadium was packed with 14,000 people, all waiting in the oppressive Southern evening heat to welcome home their home town boy made good. It was a little after ten thirty before Elvis made his entrance, sending a charge through the anticipant gathering. As was usual, the audience had been made to sit through a number of acts since eight o'clock, acts which included The Jordanaires and the Bobby Morris Orchestra. Before he started singing, Elvis was presented with an engraved scroll marking the occasion; the show was not only Elvis' homecoming, it was a charity splash from which many local causes would benefit.

In response to the presentation, Elvis thanked the compere, then turned to the audience and announced: 'I'm gonna show you what the real Elvis is like tonight!', an obvious reference to his appearance on the Steve Allen show. The 'real' Elvis was what the people of Memphis had come to see, and they were ready to show it as Elvis gave one of his best ever performances. *Mystery Train*,

Blue Suede Shoes, I Gotta Woman were all included, together with a rousing, sweat-soaked encore of *Hound Dog*. As the last notes of *Hound Dog* died, Presley took the edge of the stage, waved goodbye, and then, the first instance of something which was to become a regular feature of Presley gigs, he was surrounded by policemen, whisked out to a car, and into the night, leaving the fans screaming for more. And the Colonel selling 8 x 10s at a furious rate of knots.

Ed Sullivan, the 'big noise' of American television in the fifties and early sixties had already gone on record as saying 'I wouldn't touch Elvis Presley with a big stick', but after witnessing the Steve Allen show, and more importantly, its effect on the ratings, Sullivan was soon burning the telephone wires into the William Morris booking agency office. The agency and Colonel Parker negotiated a deal which prised out of Ed Sullivan the then princely sum of $50,000 for three shows. It was the highest fee Sullivan had ever paid.

Steve Allen contemplated bidding against Sullivan for Elvis' services, but quite correctly considered that although Elvis' appearances would send the ratings through the roof, they would be Elvis' ratings and not the show's. Allen was the first show host in the history of American television to recognise that maybe his show's success had something to do with the popularity of its guest stars rather than of its host. And it was Elvis Presley who made that truth inescapable.

From *Jailhouse Rock*, of course

Chapter Five

By the fall of 1956 the time had come for the rock 'n' roll star to look at broadening his career. September found Elvis dragging himself out of bed at 5.30 a.m. to report to the make-up department of 20th Century Fox for the day's shooting of *The Reno Brothers*, a dramatic movie set in the American Civil war.

Originally, the film was planned to be a straight drama with no songs, but the studio bosses soon figured that with Elvis Presley on hand it would be dumb, and maybe a little risky in terms of audience reaction, not to include any songs. It was a decision which didn't particularly please Elvis, as one of the attractions to him of doing a movie was the fact that it offered a dramatic role, a chance to try something new. Nevertheless, four songs were commissioned for the movie, to be inserted in appropriate places through the storyline, and the film's title was changed to that of one of the songs — *Love Me Tender*.

Ken Darby, a west coast musician, was asked to write the tunes. Darby was the leader of the Ken Darby Trio, a country and western outfit, which included in its line-up an accordian. This lent a completely different sound to the songs in the movie from that to which Elvis had been accustomed.

Elvis threw himself eagerly into the project, as was his way in those days, and on his first morning on the set he told the producer that he had not only learned his own lines, but every other part in the movie as well! Elvis felt that if the studio was willing to spend such large amounts of money on his film debut, then the least he could do was to prepare himself thoroughly.

(Interviewing J. D. Sumner many years later, I was told that, in those pre-Army days, when Elvis decided to do anything he committed himself to it body and soul. This may have been a trait that stood him in good stead professionally, but may have been the downfall of his private life.)

Although the four songs in the film were written by Ken Darby, the credits on the record labels say that they were written by Vera Matson and Elvis Presley, courtesy of the Colonel. Vera Matson was in fact Mrs Ken Darby, and the explanation behind these shenanigans reveals just one more facet of Tom Parker's restless knack for making money. When the songs for the film were submitted they were to be published by Elvis' publishing firm which belonged to BMI (Broadcast Music Inc.) while Darby himself was a member of the rival ASCAP (American Society of Composers, Authors and Publishers), so at the 'suggestion' of Parker, Darby allowed his wife and Presley to be named as composers. This way Elvis received fifty percent of the composer's royalty plus publishing income from the songs, while Darby shared royalties on four very successful tunes. Elvis was not a songwriter, but he was certainly making a lot of money from publishing and writing royalties.

On September 9, Elvis took a break from filming to appear on the Ed Sullivan show, which was then known as 'The Toast Of The Town'. Elvis' segment of the show was transmitted from Hollywood, and inserted into the New York based program. This was the big one, the nation's hottest new singer on the nation's number one TV show. That night, the Sullivan show was watched by 82.6% of the viewing public, an estimated fifty four million people — or one third of the United States (a record which stood until 1964, when it was broken by The Beatles when they appeared for Sullivan)!

Elvis sang four numbers on the show: *Don't Be Cruel*, *Hound Dog*, *Ready Teddy* and a preview of *Love Me Tender*. It was not one of his best performances, and he looked decidedly uneasy during *Love Me Tender*.

Presley's first Sullivan appearance continued the trend of sharp contrast between the reactions of audience and critics. The viewers loved him, the reviewers were scathing in their notices.

Within a week of this first Sullivan show, RCA released all seven of Elvis' previous singles simultaneously, a step which had no precedent in recording history. Billboard reported the move thus: 'Fourteen tunes, formerly available on Presley's LPs or EPs, now available on seven singles, within reach of any kid with 89 cents.' In addition, Elvis had introduced *Love Me Tender* on the show, saying that it was from his first movie, and that he hoped everybody would like it. They did, and when RCA was inundated with 850,000 orders for the single, they had to release it a week early. This made a total of eight singles simultaneously on sale!

RCA's gamble paid off; Elvis had three Number One hits in a row with *Hound Dog*, *Don't Be Cruel* and *Love Me Tender*. The fall of 1956 belonged to Elvis Presley in a way that no season had ever previously 'belonged' to a single recording star.

On September 12, 1956 Gladys Presley walked out of the kitchen at 1034, Audubon Drive, wiping her hands on her apron. 'Vernon honey, ah just don't know what we're gonna do, I can't get no sleep at night with all them kids outside the house, and the doorbell ringin' all day, ah'm so tired.' She crossed over the room to the small cocktail cabinet, took out a bottle of gin, poured a measure, and swallowed two small white pills along with the contents of the glass.

Vernon Presley watched his wife intently, and saw the tiredness in her eyes. 'Mama, don't take on so,' he replied. 'You don't need to be takin' them pills.'

'But I feel like I'm too fat honey, Elvis don't want a mama that's fat and ugly, not now he's

mixin' with all them folks and stars; the pills just help me lose a little weight, that's all.'

Vernon knew it was no use arguing with her; there was nothing she wouldn't do for Elvis. If she thought she was too fat to be the mother of a star, then nothing would dissuade her from a crash diet.

Gladys sat down on the sofa, and with a sadness in her eyes looked up at the portrait of Elvis hanging above the record player. 'You know, Vernon,' she went on, 'I wish Elvis would quit right now, marry a girl and have a child. That'd make me so happy, he's got enough comin' in from his records and stuff, he could retire right now. He could put himself in a furniture store and really mop up. If he did that, I'd be so happy.'

'Well why don't ya tell him?' Vernon asked.

Gladys peered wistfully up at the portrait then muttered: 'No, whatever makes Elvis happy is okay with me, if he's enjoyin' what he's doin', what right have I to interfere?'

She never did reveal her feelings to her son.

On October 28, Elvis was back on the Sullivan show. Again he was given four songs, *Hound Dog, Love Me Tender, Don't Be Cruel* and *Love Me*, a song new to Elvis' repertoire.

Presleymania was becoming part of the American way of life. Teenagers had found someone to identify with, and they were not about to let go. James Dean had already been removed from the scene, tragically and just as suddenly as he had arrived, and though thousands carried a torch for Dean that was kindled by the posthumous release of his final movie, *Giant*, Elvis Presley was fast taking his place as the country's teen idol of the fifties. Indeed, Elvis and Jimmy Dean had a similar appeal; Dean had awakened a sense of rebelliousness in America's post-war youth which Elvis embodied and in which he allowed teenagers to participate via rock 'n' roll music.

(James Dean, the movie star, was the first international teen hero of the post-war period. He died in a road accident in 1955, having completed just three movies.)

By now, Colonel Tom's publicity machine was firing on all cylinders. There was so much merchandise on the market bearing the Presley name, that Parker designated a firm to officially license the product and market the King's image. This practice was to become one of the most lucrative aspects of Presley's career. In 1956 one could buy such varying products as Elvis Presley lipstick in 'Hound Dog Orange', Elvis T-shirts, jeans, charm bracelets, Elvis busts, pens and pencils, stuffed animals, watches, bubblegum cards... You name it — and let your imagination be as outrageous as it wants — you could get it.

Elvis Presley Enterprises was marketing one hundred and eighty-eight products, and Parker, Presley and Hank Saperstein, head of the marketing firm, between them collected a royalty ranging from four to eleven percent of the retail price.

September 26, just prior to the second Sullivan show, found Elvis revisiting his birthplace. Tupelo, Mississippi was the venue for the Mississippi-Alabama Fair and Dairy show, and Elvis Presley was the star attraction. The small community turned out to welcome its prodigal son returned; the local High School majorettes and band headed a parade in the early afternoon, winding through Tupelo, down the main street, underneath a banner which had been hung right across the street outside the Kincannon-Elkin Co. drugstore. The banner read 'Tupelo welcomes Elvis Presley Home'. The fest was officially recognized as Elvis Presley Day.

Elvis was to perform two shows; just before the afternoon show he was presented with a three foot long key to the city made in the shape of a guitar; on it was the inscription: 'Welcome Home— Tupelo, Miss.'

The afternoon show was not a sell-out, though the local ball park was reasonably full, but there was not a spare inch around the makeshift stage on which Elvis was working. The house was crammed for the evening performance, however, with fans traveling from as far afield as Jackson, Birmingham and Alabama to catch the phenomenon that was Elvis Presley live on stage.

Elvis swirled out into the lights, hitting the crowd with *That's Alright Mama*, the National Guard had been called in as security, and pretty soon the Guardsmen found that keeping the fans from reaching the velvet shirted, sweating rock singer was no easy assignment. *Good Rockin' Tonight, Tutti Frutti, Don't Be Cruel* and the inevitable finale of *Hound Dog* — Elvis gave the fans of Tupelo the works and they loved him.

After the performance, Elvis autographed

the $10,000 cheque which was his fee, and presented it to the city of Tupelo.

November 15, 1956. New York's Paramount Theatre is besieged by hundreds of teenage fans. They line up around the ancient movie theater, blocking the streets which eventually have to be cordoned off. It is an unusual sight at any time of the day, but this is eight a.m., for chrissake! The occasion is the opening of a little movie called *Love Me Tender*, and all the signs are that it is to be a great success. Already five hundred and fifty prints of the film have been made, as against the usual two to three hundred. It has been advertised that the first two thousand fans in the line will get the choice of an Elvis scarf, lapel button or charm bracelet.

Above the marquee outside the theater there is a thirty foot cutout of Elvis playing his guitar in a scene from the film. It's an impressive sight. CBS TV news has an interviewer on the street, asking the kids in the line why they are there. His questions do little to enhance the image of CBS newsmen as intelligent human beings with the crowd. Two girls approached by the reporter can hardly control themselves; they just prattle on about the one and only Elvis: 'Well, we're gonna stay in the theater all day, we're gonna stay there till we get thrown out, there's no one as Elvis — he's just great!'

The girls are typical of the hundreds waiting to enter the theater to witness Elvis' screen transformation from Southern hillbilly to matinee idol, courtesy of Hollywood.

Love Me Tender, the movie, starred Richard Egan, Debra Paget, Robert Middleton, William and Neville Brand — not that it's remembered for their performances. The story is set in the last days of the Civil War. Elvis plays a character called Clint Reno, and he makes a remarkably good job of his debut in what must have been a totally alien environment for him. Not that many actors can look back on their screen debuts with pride, so that Clint Reno augured well for Elvis' future in tinsel town.

True to form, what the fans loved the critics detested, and Elvis-knocking became the sport of the season in the columns of some of the nation's more august publications.

The Los Angeles Times opined that Elvis: 'pales by comparison when pitted against the resonant inflections of Egan, of course, but who comes to watch Elvis act?'

The most famous quote of the day came from the Time magazine critic who wrote: 'Is it a sausage? It is certainly smooth and damp looking, but whoever heard of a 172lb sausage six foot tall? Is it a Walt Disney goldfish? It has the same sort of big, soft, beautiful eyes and long curly lashes, but whoever heard of a goldfish with sideburns? Is it a corpse? The fact it just hangs there, limp and white with its little drop-seat mouth, rather like Lord Byron in the wax museum...but suddenly the figure comes to life. The lips part, the eyes half close, the clutched guitar begins to undulate back and forth in an uncomfortably suggestive manner, and wham! The mid section of the body jolts forward to jump and grind and beat out a low down rhythm that takes its pace from boogie and hillbilly, rock 'n' roll, and something known only to Elvis and his pelvis.

'As the belly dance gets wilder, a peculiar sound emerges. A rusty foghorn? A voice? Or merely a noise produced, like the voice of a cricket, by the violent stridulation of the legs? Words can occasionally be made out, like raisins in corn meal mush. 'Goan...Git... luhhhv...' and then all at once everything stops, and a big trembly, tender half smile half sneer smears slowly across the Cinemascope screen. The message that millions of US teenage girls love to receive has just been delivered.'

The Time columnist clearly had a witty way with the words he knew millions of middle-class, middle-aged Americans wanted to read. Not that many Presley fans subscribed to Time.

Junior Smith threw the offending magazine clear across the hotel room. 'Whadda them sons-of-bitches know, anyway!' Smith was ready to explode. His mouth oozed a saliva from one of its corners, a telltale sign that Junior was getting angry. 'What's wrong with these people, Colonel?' Rarely did Elvis' cousin and traveling companion say much, but he was incensed by the Time magazine diatribe and he turned to Colonel Parker for an explanation.

'Whoa, boy,' Parker muttered, smiling and drawing his cigar. 'Lemme tell you, that picture has had five hunnerd 'n' fifty prints done on it, it's damn near took a million dollars at the box office already, and the film company are happy, so I don't know what makes them people write them kinda things, but I'll tell you sumpin' boy: I don't giva shit!'

Elvis stood, hands deep in his pockets staring moodily out of the hotel window, listening to Parker. He turned and grumbled: 'Colonel, I don't understand why they have to be so bitter toward me. I'm only doin' ma job, I'm only singin' and havin' a good time, and they're sayin' I'm dirty and obscene.' In his mind he could picture Gladys reading the things that they said about him, and his brow furrowed. 'Colonel, if I thought that I was really like they say, I would give up the business.'

The Colonel said nothing. Even Parker knew that discretion was sometimes the better part of valor, and he was getting to know the kid well enough to suspect that he meant exactly what he said.

On December 4, 1956 Sam Phillips' Sun Records studio was alive with noise and activity. Carl Perkins was back in the studio for his first session since his automobile accident nine months earlier. With him was his band, which consisted of his brothers Jay on rhythm guitar, Clayton on double bass, and W. S. 'Fluke' Holland on drums. The piano player was a little known singer/pianist who had just released a single with Sun, by the name of Jerry Lee Lewis.

The boys were happy. They had just recorded what was to be Carl's next single, a tune called *Matchbox*, and everyone sensed they had recorded a hit. 'Man, that really moved,' remarked Jerry Lee, hitting the piano keyboard with a descending scale, then finishing with a crashing chord. 'That's sure to be a hit song Carl, 'cos I'm playin' peeaner on it!'

They all laughed at Jerry's outspoken opinion of himself, and Carl was just about to say something smart back at Lewis when Sam Phillips' voice came over the intercom from the control room. 'Guys, hold it a minute, there's someone here wants to say hello — I'll bring him through.' The studio door opened and there stood Elvis and his date Marilyn Evans, a showgirl from Las Vegas whom Elvis met during his engagement at the New Frontier.

'Hi, fellas.' Elvis greeted Carl and his musicians, whom he knew of old. 'Ah've just dropped by to see what songs ah can steal.' Carl enjoyed the joke even though it was a half-serious reference to Elvis' recording Carl's *Blue Suede Shoes* while Carl himself was in hospital recovering from his accident.

Carl was happy to take the remark in good spirits.

'Man you can steal as many of my tunes as you like if you're gonna make 'em Number One,' responded Carl.

Sam Phillips moved in. 'Elvis, I'd like ya to meet a guy here who's just made a record for us, and we feel he's gonna be a big star, Jerry Lee Lewis.'

Jerry stood up and shook hands. 'Hi there,' he said. Elvis just nodded, not knowing what to say. Jerry peered at the famous visitor, thinking he was being standoffish.

'Whatcha bin doin?' Elvis turned back to Carl, asking the question to ease the tension of the moment. 'We've just bin cuttin' a new single; it's an old blues tune called *Matchbox Blues*; you know, the one by Blind Lemon Jefferson?'

Elvis smiled. 'Well, you're doin' the right thing by recording them old blues tunes, Carl. I sure got some good records with 'em.'

Elvis sat down on the piano bench which had just been vacated by Jerry, and ran his fingers over the keys. He started singing the Fats Domino hit *Blueberry Hill*. Clayton Perkins and brother Jay joined in, and in a moment Carl was putting some electric guitar licks into the accompaniment, singing along too.

The studio door was still open, and through it came the voice of Sam's assistant, Jack Clement. 'Hey man,' he shouted. 'You just ain't gonna believe who's here; I'll send him through.'

Elvis and the guys looked up. Standing there, his huge frame blocking the doorway, was Johnny Cash; behind him his smiling wife Vivian. Cash and Presley were old buddies; they had toured together in the early Sun country package shows, and they greeted each other with warmth.

'Hey, man, I caught your TV show the other night,' said Cash. 'You're a goddam star now, fella.' Cash grinned. 'Whaddya doin' here?'

Elvis explained he was home for the Christmas holidays, had dropped in to see Sam, and found Carl and Jerry in session.

Not needing an invitation, Cash joined in with Elvis and Jerry, who was by now building up steam and harmonizing along. *Will The Circle Be Unbroken*, *Island of Golden Dreams* and Cash's own *Cry, Cry, Cry* were all sung with enthusiasm by four entertainers who were obviously enjoying themselves.

Sam Phillips took Jack Clement to one side. 'Goddam it, Jack, this is too good an opportunity to waste; get the Memphis Press Scimitar on the phone, and tell 'em to get a photographer over here pronto.' It was indeed too rare a moment to miss, and the newspaper sent not only a photographer, but also reporter Robert Johnson in the cameraman's wake.

The photographer took a couple of shots of Cash, Perkins, and Jerry Lee gathered around Elvis who was still at the piano. Marilyn sat on top of the piano looking decorative. Vivian Cash reminded her husband that they had intended getting in some Christmas shopping. 'Oh sure, honey,' Cash said, reluctantly and took his leave.

Jerry, Carl and Elvis continued to sing, even though the musicians had called it a day, amid growing enthusiasm. Jack Clement slipped back into the control room and switched on the recorder. 'Ya never know what might happen,' he winked at Sam. The three singers worked their way through *Peace In The Valley*, *Down By The Riverside*, *I'm With The Crowd*, *I Just Can't Make It Myself*. Elvis offered a tongue-in-cheek impersonation of Hank Snow, then went on to imitate Bill Monroe with *Little Cabin On The Hill* and *Summertime Has Passed And Gone*.

Elvis asked: 'Y'all heard Pat Boone's new record?'

'Oh yeah, I know it,' responded Jerry.

'Well, it was written for me.' Elvis went on: 'Stayed over my house for ages, never did see it. Y'know, so much junk layin' around an' all.' At which point Elvis sang the tune, demonstrating that he would have made an excellent version if he ever had recorded it.

The session gradually broke up, Elvis made his goodbyes, and gunned the Cadillac down Union Street in the direction of Audubon Drive with Marilyn in the passenger seat.

Elvis had been back in the studios during September and in the course of a successful concentrated three day session (September 1 thru 3) he recorded thirteen songs. The songs were all excellent, and included three covers of Little Richard hits, *Long Tall Sally*, *Rip It Up* and *Ready Teddy*, an old Red Foley tune called *Old Shep*, which Elvis had first sung at the age of twelve, a couple of country and

western tunes, *When My Blue Moon Turns To Gold Again* and *How do You Think I Feel*, plus *Paralyzed, Playing For Keeps, Love Me, How's The World Treating You, Too Much* and *Anyplace Is Paradise*. All these songs were recorded at Radio Recorders Studio in Hollywood, a well known record factory to which Elvis took a liking, which accounts for the fact that his sessions there were most productive.

Elvis' second album, titled simply *Elvis*, was made up of twelve tracks, all of which came from this last session. *Elvis* was released in October 1956, and made the top spot in the album charts within two weeks.

During the Christmas period of 1956, Elvis started work on his second movie, *Loving You*. It was his first film with producer Hal Wallis, and featured a storyline written especially for the King.

Before he left for Hollywood, Elvis asked Gladys to come out to the film capital for a visit. 'Ma, I know you ain't bin feelin' too good, an' the neighbors bin gettin' ya down an' all, why don't you' n' pa come on out with me to Hollywood and get yourself away from here for a while?' Elvis was worried about his mother's health; these days it seemed she was always tired, her eyes were beginning to show signs of weariness, sunken into dark pits in her face.

'All right son, if it's what you would like, I'll call the Nichols and see if they'd like to come too.' Gladys didn't fancy the trip across America with just Vernon for company, as neither of them had traveled more than a hundred miles at one time before, so she called Carl Nichols and his wife Willy, long time friends of the Presley family.

January, 1957 found Elvis staying at the Knickerbocker Hotel in Hollywood; days before his parents' arrival he was already harrassing the management. 'My Ma and Pa are coming out to see me next week, and I want them to have the best rooms you've got, I want them to be able to look out the window and see Hollywood.'

'But Mr. Presley,' the manager interjected, 'you've already got the best the hotel can offer. You have a whole floor to yourself. I suggest we put your parents on that floor, there is plenty of room.'

'Sure,' responded Elvis. 'just as long as they're happy.'

Gladys and Vernon arrived in Hollywood and were duly impressed. Overwhelmed might be a better word; Hollywood is many things, but it certainly isn't Tupelo or even Memphis, and for all they would have noticed, Elvis could have boarded the elder Presleys in the cheapest flophouse in town.

Whenever Elvis had time off from filming he would take his parents and their companions sightseeing, and on the days he was filming, they would be guests on the film set. Gladys was so proud of her son, but she found it difficult to relate to Elvis in these strange surroundings, particularly difficult to associate him with the stars whose grand homes she'd seen on the tour of the film city.

Loving You was a Paramount picture and starred Elvis, Lizabeth Scott, Wendell Corey, Dolores Hart, James Gleason, Ralph Dumke, Paul Smith, Ken Becker and Jana Lund. The plot was a rags-to-riches story not too far removed from Elvis' own biography to date. Deke Rivers (Elvis), a young truck driver, scores a big hit at a political rally where he has come to deliver beer, but stays to sing at the insistence of his buddy and a glamorous press agent (Lizabeth Scott) by the name of Glenda Markle. Glenda and Tex Warner (Wendell Corey), the leader of the band Deke has just sung with, offer him a singing job, although they already have a girl singer, Susan Jessup (Dolores Hart).

The band makes a round of small town appearances, with Deke's popularity increasing every show. Glenda gets him to sign a personal contract for her to represent him, without letting Tex know. Though he is very much attracted to Susan, Deke becomes interested in Glenda whose publicity gimmicks soon make him a celebrity. This leads to a booking in a big theater where he discovers what being a celebrity is all about. Teenagers mob his car, and demand autographs. The theater does standing room only business.

Glenda and an agent (James Gleason) book Deke to do a one man concert in a town near Dallas, and, as a publicity stunt, they plan to buy Deke a beautiful red and white convertible matched to an equally flashy red and white stage outfit. In order to find the bread for this piece of extravagance, Glenda and Tex have to cut back on expenses. Susan's job is one of the first victims of this economy drive. As consolation, Deke drives her to her home, a farm in the country, where they have

ELVIS

a great time together. Glenda is furious and drives out to bring Deke back.

Deke becomes unhappy, and wants to return to Susan. Glenda dissuades him, their conversation ending in an embrace. During rehearsals for a big TV show which Glenda has set up for him, Deke learns from Tex that Glenda is Tex's ex-wife, and that Tex hopes they'll get back together again soon. Miserable, Deke hits the road in his old hot-rod and has the inevitable smash up. Glenda finds him unhurt, and frees him from his contract. Deke does the TV show.

With Susan beside him, Deke accepts a big TV contract and asks Tex and Glenda, who by now are planning to remarry, to represent him.

The songs in the film had been commissioned through Hill and Range (Elvis' publishing company). The company gave out the film script to all their contracted writers, with the appropriate places in the text marked where a song was to be inserted. The songwriters were invited to submit songs for any or all of the spots. In this way three or four songs would be submitted for the same spot in the film, leaving Elvis with plenty of choice.

The submitted songs were all cut as demo discs, from which Elvis and the Colonel would make their final selection.

Eventually, seven songs were used in the film, and together they made up one of Elvis' best ever film soundtracks.

January 4, 1957. In four days Elvis is due to reach the ripe old age of twenty two. However, on this day, at the still tender age of twenty one and three hundred sixty two days, Presley had an appointment back in Memphis at the Kennedy Veterans Hospital to be precise, just a stone's throw from his own home. He was slated for his pre-induction medical.

Elvis was the only potential recruit to present himself at the hospital that day, as the Army had decided that Elvis, his entourage and attendant ballyhoo, the inevitable photographers, reporters and fans would be quite enough to handle in one day, without the addition of another thirty or forty would-be draftees.

Elvis was passed A-profile physically, and mentally he was marked as 'average'.

Within hours of the medical Elvis, his musicians, his two cousins and Colonel

From January '57; Elvis and Col. Tom Parker in early, happy days.

KING

Parker boarded the New York train, bound once more for the CBS TV studios where Elvis was scheduled to make a final appearance on the Ed Sullivan show.

Two days later, Elvis left the Warwick Hotel in New York, where he has stayed overnight after his journey from Memphis. A black Cadillac limousine slid down towards the theater. 'The place is mighty quiet,' Elvis observed, looking out of the tinted back windows of the car.

'They got all the streets blocked off,' said Junior, 'we've gotta try to get ya in the side door, while Neal Matthews drives up to the front of the theatre in a big flashy car. And while all the kids is lookin' for him, we slip you in the side entrance.' Diversionary tactics were hardly new to the Presley crowd, but on the night of January 6 their ingenuity was to be put to a stern test.

The show followed the pattern of most of Elvis' TV appearances; it was a failure with most of the professional pundits and a great success with the fans who actually went out and paid dollars for Elvis' records. It was on this particular program that Elvis was shown in the legendary 'from the waist up' frame. It was assumed then by many, and has passed down as folklore that this represented some kind of censorship on Sullivan's part. But the truth was far more Machiavellian. Tom Parker had had the brainwave — which he decided to keep secret even from Elvis himself — that suggestion was a much more powerful weapon than the real thing. Accordingly, he arranged with the Sullivan show's producer that, on the rocking numbers Presley would only be shown on screen from the waist up. The TV audience would listen to Elvis singing, see him smiling and hear the studio audience going wild every other second, and would draw the conclusion that really outrageous things were happening in the studio.

A smart way to pre-sell a few thousand tickets for Elvis' next concert.

On this final Sullivan show Elvis premiered the song *Peace In The Valley*. Dressed in a gold lamé vest, black velvet shirt and black pants, he sang the song well and perfectly straight. This one performance went a long way towards healing the rift which had grown between Elvis and the parents and Church leaders of America. Many think that it was a deliberate ploy to heal this breach, but it was inevitable that Elvis would record a gospel tune sooner or later.

Sullivan tried hard to 'clean up' Elvis each time the rock star featured on the program, but Sullivan was torn between a desire not to alienate his traditionally conservative audience and record viewing ratings every time the King appeared on his show.

On this occasion not only did Elvis sing a religious song, but in his introduction Sullivan made a plea for the Hungarian relief fund in Elvis' name. 'Now ladies and gentlemen, as you probably know, after he leaves here tonight with Colonel Parker, who has done such a magnificent job as his manager, Elvis Presley goes to Hollywood to do his new Paramount picture *Running Wild* for Hal Wallis (later retitled *Loving You*). While he's out there, he's going to do a big Hungarian relief show, but because he feels too keenly, this young man feels so keenly about Hungarian relief, he urges all of us throughout the country to remember that immediate aid is needed. Long before his benefit show is put on, he wants to remind you to send in your check to your various churches, Red Cross agencies, etc.'

Elvis then sang *Peace In The Valley*. In an obvious attempt to make Elvis acceptable to the older generation, Sullivan followed up with: 'Ladies and gentlemen, in as much as he goes to the coast now for his new picture, this will be the last time we shall run into each other for a while... but wait a minute... I want to say to Elvis Presley and the country, that this is a real fine, decent boy, and wherever you go, Elvis, and the guys who accompany you over there, we want to say that we never had a pleasanter experience on our show, with a big name star, than we've had with you. You're thoroughly all right — so now let's have a tremendous hand for a very nice boy.' Sullivan always knew how to play both ends against the middle; he could justify Presley's appearances on the shows to his older audience out of one corner of his ample mouth and keep faith with the younger fans out of the other, while balancing the entire success of the program, ratings and his future in TV on the end of his nose!

After singing *Too Much*, Elvis threw in a plug for the show's sponsors, Lincoln-Mercury, when he growled to the audience: 'And we're sorry that we couldn't give each

one of you a new Lincoln, but they wouldn't sell us that many!' He finished his segment of the show with *When My Blue Moon Turns To Gold Again*.

A few days later RCA released *Too Much* backed with *Playing For Keeps*. By mid February the single had reached Number One and went on to sell an incredible eight million copies within a year of release.

On January 12, Elvis was back at the mike at the Hollywood studios of Radio Recorders. The tremendous response to *Peace In The Valley* on the Sullivan show made it a prime contender for recording at this session, and sure enough, Elvis taped it together with two other religious songs, *I Believe* and *Take My Hand, Precious Lord*.

Amongst the demos that were brought for this two day session was another Otis Blackwell tune called *All Shook Up*. Elvis took an instant liking to Blackwell's soulful rocker, and he recorded a great version of the song which was released and which subsequently dominated the chart for eight successive weeks.

In between an increasingly hectic filming schedule, Elvis made further visits to the same studios. On January 19 he recorded four more tracks, then on February 23 and 24 he cut a further seven; at the same time during various visits in February and March he recorded the songs for the *Loving You* soundtrack.

Elvis was as busy in the studios now as he had ever been in his career, and some classic tracks were etched into vinyl during this period of the King's career.

It is May 1, 1957, on the MGM sound stage, at Culver City, Los Angeles. It threatens to be one of those days when nothing'll go right when 'the boy' is impossible to deal with. Neal Matthews, one of the Jordanaires stalwarts is talking with his colleague Gordon Stoker. 'He's sure in a lazy mood this mornin',' Matthews spits, glaring in the direction of the piano where Elvis sits toying with the keys.

'I know how he feels,' responds Stoker, 'we've all bin working mighty hard, I'm plumb wore out.'

Scotty and Bill are tuning their instruments. 'Elvis give me an 'A', will ya please?' calls Moore. Elvis obliges his guitar player by fingering a key on the piano, and Scotty adjusts his big Gibson semi-acoustic.

Listlessly, Elvis takes up the 'A' note he has just played, lets it swell into a chord, slowly following it with his voice until he breaks into a gospel tune — *Known Only To Him Are The Great Hidden Secrets* — Scotty and Bill join in to test their instruments and get the feel of things. 'Hey, that's nice,' Neal Matthews whispers to his partner. 'We may as well warm up the vocal chords with him.' And the two Jordanaires amble over the piano and join in with Elvis' singing.

Within an hour, the whole group of musicians is playing, the Jordanaires are singing, and Elvis' buddies, Junior Smith, Cliff Gleaves, Red West, and Alan Fortas are all chanting along with great enthusiasm. Gordon Stokes takes a break from vocals to pull himself a Coke from the studio dispensing machine. The studio producer approaches Gordon with an indignant frown on his face. 'Would somebody mind telling me what in hell's goin' on?' he demands. 'When are you guys gonna start work?' His irritation seeps to the surface like sweat. 'We've got seven songs to get through here before we can start shootin' the film, let's get on with it, huh?'

Gordon smiles, he understands what Elvis is about. 'The man's just gettin' in the mood, he'll start soon, he always does this.'

The producer snaps back: 'Let's take a break now for lunch only please don't encourage him this afternoon if he starts singing spirituals again.'

After the break Elvis naturally sits down at the piano and starts over again. The Jordanaires sit in a corner talking and taking no notice of Elvis. He looks up. 'Hey guys, ain't ya gonna sing with me?'

It is Neal Matthews who answers: 'Well, you see Elvis, the guys at the studio here think we should be gettin' on with the film songs instead of wasting time like this singing spirituals an' all.'

Elvis straightens up from the piano, slams down the lid and barks: 'Oh yeah, do they, well they can sure as hell find someone else to sing 'em.' He turns petulantly, motioning his buddies to follow him, and strides out of the studio.

Colonel Parker stares up at Freddie Bienstock, the head of Hill and Range songs, and pronounces quietly: 'Go make a phone call, and get Steve Scholes out here tomorrow. He knows how Elvis works; these guys are gonna

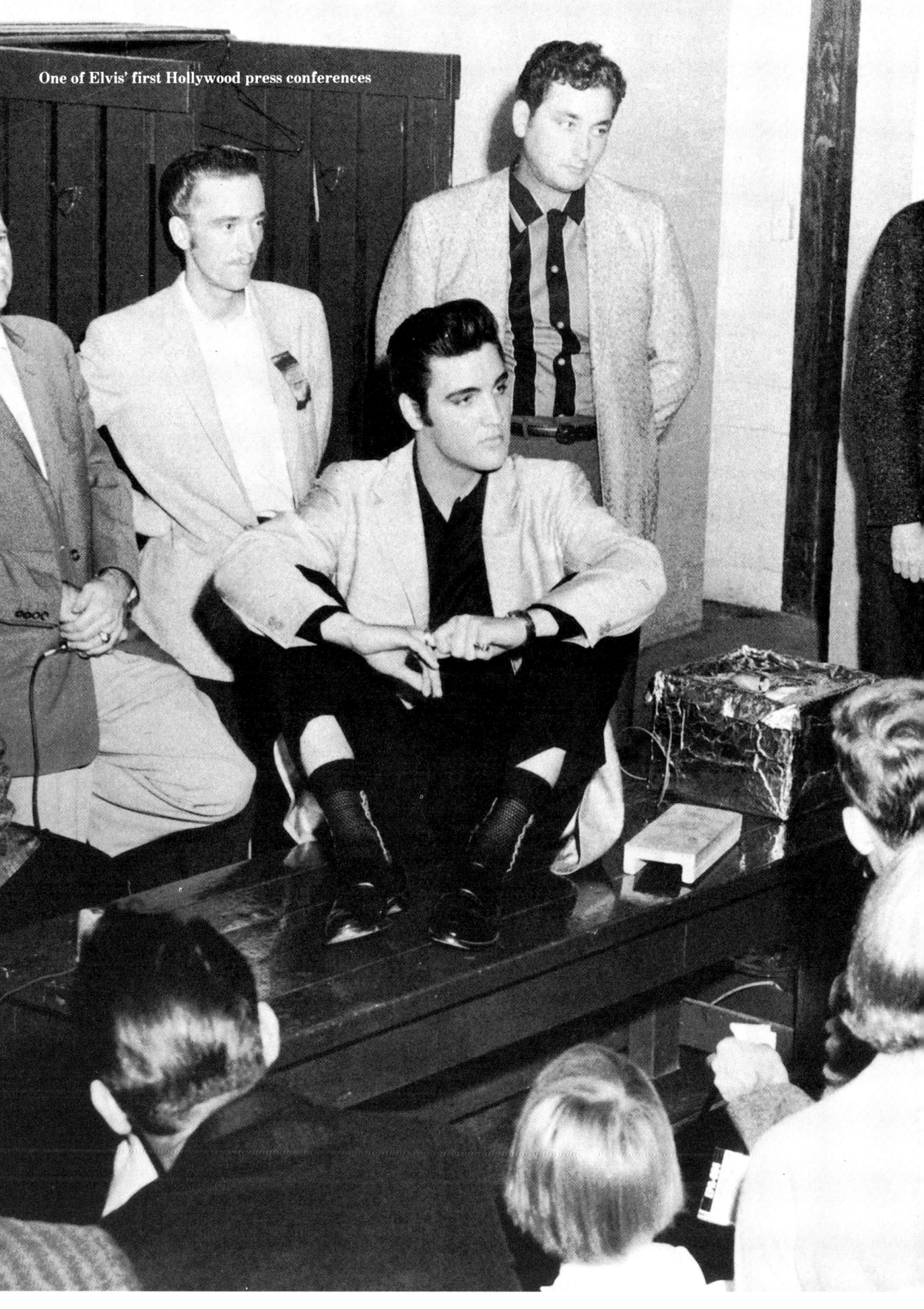
One of Elvis' first Hollywood press conferences

blow it.'

The following morning, with Steve Scholes in charge, the session gets truly under way and in the space of two days Elvis waxes the soundtrack songs for a new movie, *Jailhouse Rock*.

The film itself was directed by Richard Thorpe, produced by Pandro S. Berman, with a screenplay by Guy Trosper. After the bright color of *Loving You* the new film is back to black and white. Elvis retained the jet black hair which had been dyed for the previous film, though he had dispensed with the mascara on his eyes.

The plot is by far the most dramatic of Elvis' three films to date though no one allows plausability to get in the way of entertainment. *Jailhouse Rock* is the story of Vince Everett (Elvis), a building site laborer who stops off on May day for a drink in a bar. An argument flares up over a woman at the bar which ends in Vince knocking out his opponent. In the incident the man falls heavily, cracking his head and sustaining injuries which kill him. Vince is sent to the slammer.

In prison he shares a cell with Hunk Houghton (Mickey Shaughnessy), a former country and western singer. At first Hunk plays tough with Vince, but as time passes he allows Vince to play his guitar and after a while Vince starts singing to himself.

A television special is broadcast from the prison; Hunk and Vince both feature in it and Vince receives a tremendous number of letters after his performance. However, Hunk persuades the mail department to keep quiet about the deluge of fan mail until he has signed Vince to a contract providing that when they leave prison they will become a team and share the profits. Vince thinks he has nothing to lose, so he signs.

Vince is paroled before Hunk, and on the day of his release discovers the truth about the mail which is given to him. With his ambitions fired, Vince goes to a club looking for a job as a singer, and is offered a job, as a busboy! He enters into conversation with a girl who turns out to be an exploitation girl for a record company. She introduces herself as Peggy Van Alden (Judy Tyler). Determined to show Peggy what he can do, Vince jumps up on stage to sing; but he impresses no one and is reduced to smashing his guitar on a table in front of the only customer who has reacted in any way to Vince's performance — by laughing.

any way to Vince's performance — by laughing.

Peggy remains interested nevertheless (exactly why is the kind of question the movie's producer prefers fans not to ask) and persuades Vince to make a demo tape which they take to the head of the record company she works for. At first the boss refuses, then suddenly accepts the recording. The record is released, Peggy and Vince rush to the nearest record store to listen to it, only to discover that the recording company have stolen the song and arrangement and put it out by the big act on the label. As if record companies would stoop to such foul play! Vince is furious and punches the record company boss.

Peggy and Vince decide that the only thing to do is to start a record company of their own. They do handle everything themselves, including the marketing and distribution. During all this of course Peggy falls in love with Vince, but he is oblivious to her advances. Eventually Vince makes it big, and is making a lot of money, then Hunk is released from prison and claims his fifty percent.

Vince settles out of court for ten percent and Hunk becomes a hanger on. After much wheeling and dealing through which Vince shows himself to be a thoroughly unlikeable character, things come to a head when Vince sells the record company without telling Peggy. Hunk takes exception to this and beats Vince up, hitting him in the throat thus causing the loss of his voice. After surgery in hospital, Hunk makes up with Vince who makes up with Peggy, and everyone is about to live happily ever after but... the crunch question is, will Vince ever sing again? The clichéd ending comes with Vince nervously testing his voice, with just a friend playing piano, he starts singing *You're So Young And Beautiful* and as his confidence soars so does his voice. Enter Peggy from the other room where she has been listening, and everyone is all smiles as the closing credits roll.

The title song, *Jailhouse Rock*, became a rock 'n' roll classic. It was not just a song, it was a production number sung in the film during the TV show sequence. Elvis' natural stage movements had been captured and choreographed into a superb visual experience. Hell, the song alone was brilliant, but when coupled with this visual work it became a moment of magic, and a masterpiece of fifties musical cinema.

It was May 14, and Elvis was shooting this energetic part of the film, when suddenly he stopped, grasping his throat. 'Hold it, fellas,' he coughed and spluttered, 'I think I've swallowed a bug.' The extras and musicians all laughed, until they noticed that as he smiled it was obvious that one of Elvis' porcelain caps was no longer in his mouth. After much searching, which failed to turn up the missing cap, Elvis realized that he had swallowed the thing. 'Makes no difference, it'll come out in the same way as everything else,' he laughed, and they went back to work and finished the sequence.

The morning after, at make up, Elvis started experiencing chest pains. As a precaution he was taken down to the Cedars of Lebanon hospital where an X-ray revealed that Elvis had not swallowed but inhaled the cap and it was lodged in his lung. After an operation to remove the offending object, Elvis rested for two days then returned to the set of *Jailhouse Rock*.

Once he had finished shooting the film, Elvis took three weeks off as a summer vacation. This gave him ample time to survey the construction work which was just being completed at his latest and most expensive acquisition...Graceland.

In mid-March, Elvis and his mother had been to look at Graceland, which could best be described as a small mansion in the style of which rich Southerners are so fond. It was built of tan Tennessee limestone and boasted a beautiful white pillared façade. The house was owned by a Mrs Ruth Brown Moore whose late husband had named the house after his wife's aunt.

Graceland had not been lived in for a number of years, and it was badly in need of repair. The house was situated in what was then Whitehaven, Mississippi (a suburb of Memphis, which is now part of the city) in thirteen acres of land, high on a hilltop. The need for a new and more private residence had become a necessity; Audubon Drive had by then become almost impossible to live in, thanks to the combined problems of neighbors and fans.

On March 19, as Elvis signed the deeds for the purchase of Graceland he remarked that it 'sure needs a lot of work'.

On his return to Memphis in the summer of '57, Presley found that most of the work he had ordered on Graceland had been done; a carport had been installed and a swimming pool built, and the house had been finished to his liking with such decor as purple walls with gold trimmings, white shag pile carpets throughout, velvet curtains electrically operated, and an imitation sky in the entrance hall, which gave an impression of clouds during the day, and twinkled with lights imitating stars at night.

The whole exterior of the house was floodlit by pale blue lights; Elvis soon added the famous 'musical' gates, electrically operated, which had become a necessity. The gates were fashioned out of wrought iron with two figures of the King moulded into the design, trimmed with musical notes to finish off the effect. Twenty-five years later these gates have become almost as instantly recognisable as their famous owner, and nowadays represent the goal for the pilgrimages of many thousands of fans from all over the world.

Elvis installed his Uncle Travis Smith and Uncle Vester Presley as custodians of the gates, which were electrically operated from a gatekeeper's hut within the walls of Graceland.

When Elvis needed relaxation he would rent amusement parks, rollerskating rinks, and football fields at night, for the exclusive use of his buddies and their girlfriends. The Presley entourage would ride, rollerskate or play football as the mood dictated. Many of the games that were played on these nights were particularly rough, and most were invented by Elvis. One of the most popular, played on roller skates, was called 'war' and involved two teams of ten, who lined up opposite each other at either end of an ice rink. The rules were simple and pretty basic: the last skater standing was the winner, with no holds barred in the efforts of one team to line the playing surface with the prostrate bodies of the other. It was a rough-and-tumble sport from which many of the guests were liable to emerge battered and bruised. The host, however, usually emerged unscathed, protected from the fury by his 'minders', a rapidly growing ubiquitous group of heavies, who took upon themselves the onerous responsibility of insuring that Elvis came away from such hellraising nights in one piece.

In August 1957, the Elvis Presley travelling road show left Chicago Station and headed up the North West Pacific coast for the Canadian border, destined for Vancouver. After that there would be a triumphant return to Mississippi, then a sweep across country to Hollywood where Elvis would perform two shows in front of a star-studded audience.

Elvis' entourage had grown dramatically since those early days on the road; the train passengers included Scotty, Bill, and D. J. plus the Jordanaires as usual, but non-performing 'staff' included Alan Fortas, Lamar Fike, Red and Sonny West, Cliff Gleaves, and the cousins Gene and Junior Smith. Colonel Parker's right hand man Tom Diskin often talked to Elvis about the problem of taking so many guys on the road with him. Elvis didn't consider it strange: 'Tom, if ah've gotta make these long trips, ah like the guys with me, they remind me of home, and they look after me. Hell, Red's always fightin' some guy off who wants to bop me one, and Alan's all right...ya know how it is, Tom...the guys are okay.'

Tom never harped on the matter. If that's what the boy wanted...!

Colonel Parker was in his element on these tours; it was almost like the old carnival days, traveling a day ahead of the show in his own private railroad car, setting up the shows, then awaiting the arrival of the Elvis Presley 'circus'.

Things had certainly changed since those early dates on the road with Scotty and Bill, the endless miles in the old beat up Cadillac. Elvis found his mind wandering back to the dusty Tennessee trails, the small school house and barns of a couple of years before.

On the ride to Vancouver, Presley looked in the mirror in his compartment as the train rattled over the Canadian border, and he pondered the image. Black greasy hair, the droopy eyelids, and the mouth which naturally dropped at each corner until his little half smile forced open one side to expose his expensive dental work. 'Man, if they could only see me now, them goddamn freaks at High School who called ME a freak! We sure showed them a thing or two!' The thoughts brought an irresistable, wide grin to his face as he ran a comb through the famous locks for the hundredth time that afternoon.

Right: **Scenes from** *King Creole.*

ELVIS

On August 31, 1957 Vancouver's Empire Stadium was preparing to play host to a legend in the making; a stadium where just three years earlier athletes Roger Bannister and John Landy had broken the four minute mile in the quadrennial Empire Games, but now a star of a different game awaited his turn. Elvis was nervously pacing his dressing room, checking last minute details with Scotty and Bill and D. J.. Colonel Parker stuck his head around the dressing room door. 'Elvis, are you about ready for these press guys...do you wanna come into the other room now?'

Elvis was greeted warmly by the gathered pressmen waiting to interview him; he sat in a crouching position on a wooden table, positioned so that he could look over the heads of the newsmen and see Colonel Parker standing at the end of the room.

The newsmen and women were friendly and orderly and asked questions about anything and everything. That press call was typical of hundreds that Presley endured in those early years: a crude mix of banal and probing questions, all fielded with Presley's curious blend of deference and ingenuousness.

'Elvis, have you any records coming out that we haven't heard yet?'

'Yes, the theme song from my next picture will be out about the middle of next month.

'What is the picture?'

'*Jailhouse Rock.*'

'That's a single 45?'

'Yes.'

'How did you find Hal Wallis as a producer/director?'

'A very...ah...very fine gentleman.'

'Did he help you out, who was the big aid in your show *Loving You*?

'Well..ah...there's nobody helps you out... you have a director and a producer, and as far as the acting and as far as the singing an' all you're on your own, nobody tells ya how to do that, you have to learn it yourself.'

'How you rate yourself as an actor?'

'Pretty bad; that's something you learn through experience. I might accomplish something at it through the years.'

'Do you think it's just for the sake of acting natural — don't you do that?'

'In some scenes I was pretty natural, in others I was tryin' to act, and when you start trying to act you're dead.'

'Would you say the Jordanaires helped you a lot in your career with your songs, backing you up?'

'Well...ah...they have done a very fine job, the Jordanaires have, but actually there are a lot of groups, very fine groups that back people up on their records.'

'They are under contract to Capitol, are they not?'

'Yes.'

'I know you're under a terrific strain after a show, what tapers you down, what relaxes you after a big show like tonight?'

Well, take for instance last night: we had a big show, and I didn't sleep any till about ten o'clock today, I get all keyed up and I ah...it's tough to relax.'

'Whaddya do before a show?'

'I just walk around and, uh, swallow, and clench ma fists.'

'How much did you pay for that guitar?'

About five hundred dollars.'

'Is it specially constructed or is it the standard model?'

'No, it's a standard guitar; I have a leather cover over it, I had that made.'

'Do you find that making movies is much more hard on you than touring or TV shows?'

'Touring is the roughest part, it's really rough, because I mean, you're in a town, you do a show, you come off, you ride in a car, you go on to the next town.'

'Would you prefer more to making movies and doing TV or would you rather stick to movies and records?'

'I think every performer likes to work to a live audience.'

'How was the weather down in Memphis before you left, were you in Memphis before coming here?'

'Yes I was home — it was beautiful weather.'

'Why did you have the Great Northern train stop two miles outta town today and stop an' get out there?'

Elvis wasn't sure how to answer this question; he shot a glance at Colonel Parker, and muttered 'Planning!' Parker mumbled something about the fans, and Elvis took up the conversation again. 'You see, I had to prepare for a show that night, and therefore I had to rest. We had rehearsals in the afternoon, so I didn't have too much time. I'm

Main Photo: with Vic Morrow in *King Creole*

actually pressed for time; it's not that I'm trying to avoid anyone, it's just that I'm rushed for time, and I have to make every moment count when I'm on the road.'

'Can you make faster time into town in your Cadillac than you can on the train?'

'Actually you're tryin' to trap me now. I don't know what to say! Ah...next?'

'You've been through a lot of interviews Elvis; which question do you dislike the most?'

'I don't know, like I said, I've been asked everything, if they're too rough, I just, ah, I can't answer 'em.'

'How do you feel about being asked questions about your personal life?'

'Well, let's face the facts, anybody that's in the public eye, their life is never private ya know; I mean everything you do the public knows about it. That's the way it's always bin, and that's the way it'll always be.'

'Elvis, you've been on the road for a long, long time and it's about time you had a nice big rest because you deserve it; where would you like to go for a holiday somewhere?'

'Africa!...ah, no...I don't know, there's a lotta places I'd like to go.'

'Have you considered a holiday, you've been on the go for what, two years now, about a year an' a half?'

'About four years.'

'Four years! — well this throws a different light on things altogether. What happened four years ago, did you get your start four years ago?'

'Yes.'

'Where?'

'In Memphis.'

'Is that when the first record came out?'

'Yes.'

'What was it: *That's Alright Mama*, or something else?'

'Yeah, that's the name of it. Actually no, I wasn't known at all until Colonel Parker started managing me, and I got on RCA Victor, and on television, and then I started being known.'

'Before that time you were recording on the Sun label for Sam Phillips?'

'Yes, I was known in certain sections you know, but I wasn't known all over.'

'The record, was it Dewey that played the first one, is he related to the other Phillips in any way?'

'No they're no kin; he says he was the first time, I don't know!'

'Do you want to go overseas someday, Elvis?'

'Yes, I would like to; I would like to.'

'What are your thoughts on permanent retirement?'

'I'd like to!' (This brings gales of laughter from the pressmen.)

'Retirement? — well put it like this, I'll never quit as long as I'm doin' okay.'

'Whaddya consider doin' okay?'

'Well, as long as you're pleasing the people, it'd be foolish to quit.'

'When you get caught in a bar or something, have you ever been seriously hurt by the girls?'

'Yes. I've been scratched...bitten and everything.'

'What do you think about it?'

'Well, I just accept it with a broad mind, because actually they don't intend to hurt ya, I mean it's not that, they just want pieces of you for souvenirs.'

'Elvis, you've got a big crowd out here tonight. What do you consider to be your best crowd, whaddya consider your favorite place?'

'I have no favorite place; probably the biggest crowd was in Dallas, Texas last year. Yes, I played The Cotton Bowl: I had 32,000 people there.'

'What is that stone in the beautiful ring on your left hand?'

'It's a star sapphire. A girl gave that to me in California.'

'Where do you go for a quiet cuppa coffee nowadays?

'When I'm traveling around I don't go anywhere, I just eat in ma room.'

'When do you head out to the army, Elvis?'

'I haven't heard from them, I don't know yet.'

'How do you like the motion picture field, Elvis?'

'I think it's great, I like it better than any phase of the business, other than the public appearances.'

'You'd rather be in movies than sing, shall we say?'

'Well...ah, no I'm not gonna say that.'

'Why don't we see more of you on television, seeing as you can command such big fees?'

'I don't know. I guess Colonel Parker could answer that.'

'Don't ya get tired of newsmen and cameramen all the time, Elvis?'

'No, I don't mind 'em.'

'Do you think the rock 'n' roll craze is dying, Elvis?'

'No sir, I don't think it's dying; I'm not saying that it won't die, but I don't think it is right now.'

'Elvis, who would you say was responsible for your great success in the music field. I mean, getting your big start away. Where did you get your start, was it in western music that you started?'

'How did Hank Snow fit into the picture, if he did?'

'Well, at the time that I started singing, Colonel Tom Parker was managing Hank Snow, and that's how we got connected, I don't know why Hank and my name were linked together so much, 'cos actually we wasn't connected in any way in business; I just worked on some o' Hank's personal appearances.'

'Do you know his son?'

'Yeah, Jimmie Rodgers Snow, yeah.'

'Did you ever pal around with him or anything?'

'Yes, quite a bit.'

'Elvis, is your first love western music?'

'No sir, it's not, my ah...my first I would say would be spiritual music.'

'Like *Peace In The Valley* and that?'

'Not exactly that, some of the old colored spirituals, you know, from years back.'

'Elvis, your actions make quite a reaction in the audience, what is your opinion of the audience?'

'Well, I mean it would look pretty funny out there without one! Actually, I suppose you're talking about all the yelling and what not; actually, it's good 'cos it covers up my mistakes, whenever I hit a sour note nobody knows it but me!'

'If everything folded up tomorrow, what would you do?'

'Go back to drivin' a truck.'

'Do you like drivin' a truck?'

'No, I don't know what I'd do, that's counting your chickens before they hatch. Actually, I'd like to learn a lot about acting.'

'Are you happier now, or were you happier when you were drivin' a truck and you could have a quiet cup o' coffee?'

'Well, I'm happier now in a lotta ways, but I mean I was havin' a lot of fun then, you know.'

The interview over, Elvis passed time in his dressing room. A caged thoroughbred waiting to leave the starting gate, Presley would be dressed in a magnificent 'gold' jacket with rhinestone lapels and cuffs, part of an incredible suit which had been made especially for him on this trip by the famous Hollywood tailor, Nudie — well known for some of the more eccentric costumes sported by the top country music performers. The suit was made to look like gold leaf, but it was actually thin leather sprayed gold, and looked rather big for Elvis. Still, it set Elvis and the Colonel back a princely $10,000. Elvis had damaged the trousers at an earlier show, so he was wearing the jacket over a black shirt and black trousers.

Elvis was worrying about his entrance to the stadium. Colonel Parker had arranged for a white Cadillac convertible to pick the singer up at the dressing room, then circle the running track with Elvis perched on the back waving to the crowds until he reached the 'stage', which was in fact the flat bed of a truck set up at one end of the field.

'I sure hope none of them kids git over the fence while we're drivin' round the place,' Elvis said to Red West. 'Either I'm gonna get hurt or some o' them are.' He was genuinely worried about the safety of the Colonel's showstopping plan.

Out in the stadium, the audience, a mass of humanity around 25,000 strong which had paid a total of $44,000 to see the star, were being 'entertained' by a bill that instantly and bizarrely exposed the Colonel's carney background: the Burns Twins and Evelyn — tap dancers! Joe Termini — a comedy violinist; Wells and the Four Fays — acrobats; Paul Desmond — impressionist and, of course, the inevitable Jordanaires. Parker was content to let the audience's frustration build, heat it up to fever pitch before bringing Elvis on stage.

The interval came and passed, and the big moment had arrived. The white Cadillac left the dressing room area and moved off around the track, with Elvis on the back. The kids strained at the wire fence separating them from their idol, and the Royal Canadian Mounted Police wore worried looks.

Elvis reached the makeshift stage already occupied by Scotty, Bill, D.J. and the Jordanaires, and he climbed the steps at the back, catapulting into the spotlight with the opening bars: 'Weeell, since ma baby left me...'

The audience went wild.

Moving straight into *That's Alright, Mama*, with just enough time to pick up his beautiful leather cased Gibson guitar which he had used in *Loving You*, the man wiggled across the stage.

After about fifteen minutes of Elvis's scheduled thirty minutes, Scotty walked over to Bill between numbers and out of the side of his mouth said 'Do you see what I see?'

Bill did. 'Them sonnabitches is gettin' closer!'

The fans at the far end of the stadium decided they were too far away, and started edging forward, over the perimeter fence and onto the field. The mounties allowed them over the fence thinking that they could contain them beyond the twenty yard line. Unfortunately, the other kids around the stadium, on seeing this, were afraid they were going to miss out, so they climbed the fence too. In a few short minutes the whole field in front of the stage was engulfed by fans, and the iron safety fence in front of the stage was in danger of collapse.

Gordon Stoker looked across at Elvis, realising the danger. Elvis was still dancing along the front of the stage, teasing and tantalising the kids. 'Elvis,' Stoker shouted, 'get the hell outta here — we're gonna get killed!'

Still performing, Elvis danced his way to the back of the stage near the steps. When he reached them he said to the musicians: 'I'm cuttin' out, man.'

The boys needed no gilt-bordered invitation — they fled. Scotty rescued his guitar, and Bill his double bass, but the rest of the equipment was lost under the feet of rampaging fans.

It took two hours for them to get out of the stadium that night.

By September 26, 1957 the Elvis Presley show was on board train again, heading for Tupelo, Mississippi. Elvis and his team were to appear there the following day in another benefit show, this time for the 'Elvis Presley Youth Recreation Center' to be built by the Tupelo City Council with aid from the man himself.

There were sounds of an argument coming from Tom Parker's compartment. Parker was sat facing Scotty Moore and Bill Black, with Elvis at his right hand. He was annoyed.

With Johnny Cash, a compatriot from the Sun days

'Scotty you've done real well outta this deal, you ain't gone short.'

Scotty almost exploded: 'Shit, Colonel, we've gotta pay our own rail fare and hotel bills outta our salary, it's not like Elvis ain't makin' the money now; all I'm askin' is a $50 a week raise with a cash payment of $10,000 to git ma debts sorted.'

(Scotty and Bill received a hundred dollars a week when they were at home, and two hundred when they were on the road, plus a thousand dollar bonus at Christmas.)

Elvis looked at the Colonel not knowing just what to say.

Parker took the cigar from his mouth, and pointed the stub at Scotty's chest. 'Who in fuck do ya think ya are? Askin' for $10,000, you're only a goddam hillbilly guitar player, there's plenty more where you came from.'

Elvis shuffled his feet and looked at Bill in exasperation.

Bill was calm. 'Elvis, we've bin on the road together now for four years, don't that mean nuthin' to ya? Are we not worth an extra fifty a week?'

'Bill, it ain't that,' Elvis replied. 'I don't see ma money, you know that, the Colonel handles it. What can ah do?'

Scotty butted in. 'You can tell this sonnabitch here' — indicating Parker — 'that you want us to play for ya, and that you're gonna pay us more money. For Chrissake Elvis, it's your show.'

'Scotty, gimme a couple o' days to sort it out, will ya?' Elvis asked.

'But you've already had a week to think about it!' said Scotty. 'Look, man, we quit!'

Scotty and Bill left the compartment. Elvis looked at the Colonel.

'Look boy, you're the star, an' there ain't nobody holdin' a gun to ma head an gittin' away with it, ah tell ya, boy!'

'But it was ma head, Colonel,' said Elvis softly, and he holed up in his compartment for the rest of the journey.

Scotty and Bill didn't appear with Elvis the following day. Instead the Colonel sent for Hank Garland, a noted young Nashville guitar player, and Bob Moore, another Nashville man who played bass.

On their return to Memphis, Scotty and Bill were interviewed by the local press, and Scotty said: 'I didn't expect to get rich on this, and I certainly don't begrudge him the success he's had or what it brought him, but I did expect to do better than that. At one time Elvis wanted to put himself and Bill on a quarter percent royalties of every record sold, but it never got put on paper.

Had this gesture ever been formalized, it would have made millionaires of both musicians. A quarter percent may not sound much, but a quarter percent of some of the most successful hit recordings, movie soundtracks and TV shows in the history of popular music certainly would have piled up the bucks. Scotty and Bill never returned to Elvis' payroll, but their anger and disappointment subsided enough for them to be hired if and when Elvis needed them. Parker may have figured he could do without them, but Elvis wanted the boys to work with him, so the manager had to grin and bear a compromise with his young 'property'.

Scotty and Bill were reunited with Elvis a lot quicker than they expected. In late September '57, the Elvis Presley stage show rolled into Hollywood for two prestige shows at the Pan-Pacific Auditorium. This was Elvis Presley as high in his career as he had ever been, or was ever to reach again. His third film, *Jailhouse Rock*, had just opened, the soundtrack album from the film *Loving You* was Number One in the album charts, *Teddy Bear* was still in the Top Ten, and the *Peace In The Valley* extended play was in the EP charts.

The Colonel strode into Elvis' dressing room before the first show. 'Man, there's 9,200 people out there and they've all paid, every damn last one of 'em — I've even made the press an' radio folks pay for their tickets!'

Elvis smiled. It was totally unheard of to make the newspaper critics and radio people pay to come and see a show — after all they were the folks you wanted on your side — but pay they had, and the total ticket take came to a staggering $56,000 for two performances in two nights. 'Colonel, I don't know how you do it,' Elvis remarked.

'Well, son, you jus' leave the money to the 'ol Colonel here and you jus' git on out there an' give 'em a show. I want you to give the best show you've ever given tonight.'

'I always do Colonel,' was Elvis' surprised answer.

'Well, I know that Elvis, but tonight I want ya to go a little wild, ya know? Give 'em your best shots, give 'em somethin' to talk about, there's some influential people out there

tonight. They've come to see what all this talk about bein' a 'dirty' singer is about. We'll show 'em; I wanna see your name all over them newspapers in the mornin'.'

The audience sat through the same acts who had accompanied Elvis in Canada and down in Mississippi, and waited through the interval, which Colonel Parker's men turned to good advantage by selling photos and programs. After the intermission it was time for the man to take the stage and, taking the Colonel at his word, he gave the audience something to watch. Dressed in the same gold jacket, black shirt and black pants, he used every trick in the book, bits of business that by now were second nature to him. Elvis knew when to approach the front of the stage, when to sing a slow song, when to launch into a hot rocker, when to drop on one knee, when to prostrate himself across the stage. He drove 'em wild, ending one number by sitting astride a model of RCA's trademark dog, 'Nipper'.

The following afternoon, Elvis and the Colonel were sat having their first meal of the day in the Knickerbocker Hotel, when a waiter came to tell Parker he was wanted on the phone. The Colonel left the newspaper he was reading open at the page which carried a review of the previous evening's show, a piece peppered with words like 'sexhibitionist', and 'contrived sensual gestures', comparing Elvis' concert unfavorably with 'one of those screeching uninhibited party rallies which Nazis used to hold for Hitler'.

When the Colonel returned he was grinning.

'You look pleased, Colonel,' said Gene Smith.

'Naw, it ain't that, you just gotta laugh, it seems that we started sumpin' a little more than just newspaper reviews last night. That was the Los Angeles police department on the phone, it seems they think you're doin' somethin' you shouldn't oughtta with little 'Nipper!'.

Elvis looked dumbfounded, 'Whadd'ya mean, Colonel?'

'Well, to put it straight to ya, son, they thought that you were simulatin' sex with that little 'ol dog.' The Colonel bust out laughing, what with that crazy thought in his head and the sight of Elvis' genuinely perplexed face he couldn't control himself. Presley took it hard. He didn't want anybody

thinking things like that; he'd acted spontaneously on stage the previous evening, not meaning any harm.

The Colonel meanwhile was in seventh heaven. 'They're even sending down some film cameras to shoot tonight's show in case you get up to anything else. What publicity!'

That night Elvis hit the stage with *Heartbreak Hotel*. After he had finished, he looked across at the camera belonging to the cops and muttered: 'I wonder if they're gonna release this in the theaters? Turning to the audience, he announced, 'I'm sorry this came up, but we're not gonna let it stop us from puttin' on a good show tonight for you people. If they think it's obscene then that's their problem, not mine!' Smiling broadly, he continued: 'I'm gonna be an angel tonight.' Joking aside, Elvis took the hint and toned his performance down slightly; no matter that the Colonel relished the free publicity; Presley didn't want to get a reputation for obscenity.

On December 20, 1957, Milton Bowers, the draft board chairman delivered Elvis' draft papers in person to Graceland where Elvis had retired for the Christmas holidays. The world's first rock 'n' roll star was due to report to the Memphis draft board office on January 20, 1958.

CHAPTER SIX

In mid November 1957, RCA released the long-player *Elvis' Christmas Album*, and immediately the singer was clouded in further controversy. While the album included cuts like Gene Autrey's *Here Comes Santa Claus* and Irving Berlin's standard *White Christmas*, plus a bunch of new songs such as *Santa Claus Is Back In Town* by Jerry Leiber and Mike Stoller, and *Santa Bring My Baby Back To Me* by Aaron Schroeder and Claude Demetrius, it also featured a number of traditional carols, which is where the problems lay.

It was the inclusion of *O Little Town Of Bethlehem* and *Silent Night* which seemed to upset a lot of dyed-in-the-wool radio stations. Many of these stations refused to play anything from the album at all, opining that it was 'blasphemous' and 'in bad taste'. Christmas carols were not designed to be sung by a young rock 'n' roller who, they said, did all manner of disgusting things on stage.

Nevertheless, the album was a runaway commercial success, and remains today one of the most sought-after records by collectors of Presley's vintage product.

Meanwhile at Paramount Pictures, panic was setting in — to put it mildly. The studio had invested between $300,000 and $350,000 on Elvis' next picture and, if he entered the army before March 1958, the money would be lost, along with quite a few million in anticipated box-office receipts.

The Paramount chiefs sent a letter to the draft board asking for an eight week extension; military service couldn't be allowed to interfere with company profits, surely the draft board could see that. The draft board replied coolly that any request of that nature would have to come from the draftee himself.

Elvis wrote to the board somewhat reluctantly, explaining that Paramount had been good to him in his early days, and that he felt that he owed it to the studio to insure that 'the nice folks wouldn't lose so much money'.

The three man draft board held a meeting, and agreed to defer Elvis' entry into the army by sixty days, giving him a new reporting date of March 20.

Milton Bowers, the head of the draft board, was to regret that decision, which provoked a great deal of criticism from many quarters. On the one hand he was besieged by the letters and phone calls of irate Elvis fans, complaining that the King's drafting would deprive them of his music and was all some sinister Establishment plot; on the other, Bowers was in trouble with war veterans, civic leaders, mayors and State representatives for giving Elvis 'preferential treatment' by allowing him a deferment for the unseemly purpose of making money for a film studio.

Many of the letters and phone calls were bitter and threatening, some were humorous, but hardly any condoned the board's decision.

There was no way that Bowers could win, and after stating he was 'fed up to the teeth with Elvis Presley' he opined in the newspapers that: 'With all due respect to Elvis, who's a nice boy, we've drafted people who are far, far more important than he is. After all, when you take him out of the entertainment business, what have you got left? — a truck driver!'

In January, 1958 Elvis and his entourage once again boarded a train leaving Memphis station, bound for Hollywood. This time the journey was different; every station and small town halt that the train passed through was lined with fans anxious for a final glimpse of this strange new phenomenon before he disappeared into the armed forces. The reception at most places was so great that Elvis took to standing at the rear of the train on the observation platform, so that he could get a better view of the crowds, and they of him.

Elvis was genuinely overwhelmed at this show of feeling from the people. 'Man, I don't know what to say,' he stuttered to Tom Diskin. 'I never thought that folks would just come and wave at a train.'

'They know, Elvis, that it's the last time for two years that they're gonna get a chance to see ya,' explained Diskin.

'Yeah, I know,' Elvis replied, suddenly subdued. He sat down and went quiet. 'Two years is a long time, Tom; they gonna forget me by the time I git out the Army, man it's gonna have to be the movies for me from now on.'

'Well, you know, Elvis,' Diskin said, 'the Colonel will be lookin' out for you while you're in the forces. What with the new picture an' all, and the records you've cut and ain't released yet, things'll work out all right you'll see. Trust the Colonel.'

During January and early February Elvis worked on the film *King Creole* in Hollywood; between time on the set he went into Radio Recorders studio to tape the sound track songs, which were among the best movie songs he's ever recorded.

The title song was another Jerry Leiber/ Mike Stoller classic; the same team were responsible for *Trouble*, one of the highlights of the film, and for *Steadfast, Loyal And True* one of its more forgettable musical moments. Aaron Schroeder was again on hand, and he wrote or co-wrote *Dixieland Rock* and *Young Dreams*. Syd Tepper and Roy Bennett wrote the bluesy *New Orleans*;, while Fred Wise and Ben Weisman were responsible for *Don't Ask Me Why* and *As Long As I Have You*. The remaining song, the catchy *Lover Doll* was the work of Sid Wayne.

King Creole was based on Harold Robbins' book *A Stone For Danny Fisher* in which the

With George Klein, a Memphis DJ and close friend. Klein was one of the bearers at Elvis' funeral.

hero was a boxer based in New York. For the purposes of the film the main character was changed to that of a singer (naturally) and the location was changed to New Orleans.

The cast for this film was as strong as any that had graced Elvis' films to date, and included Carolyn Jones, Dolores Hart, Dean Jagger, Liliane Montevecchi, Walter Matthau, Jan Sheperd, Paul Stewart and Vic Morrow. Hal Wallis produced, and Michael Curtiz directed. According to the storyline it's the last day of school for Danny Fisher (Elvis), as he heads to his early morning job at the Blue Shade, a cheap nightclub on Bourbon Street in New Orleans' French Quarter.

There an all-night drinking party is in progress and, after being forced to sing a song, he rescues Ronnie (Carolyn Jones) from a pawing hoodlum. Ronnie, property of racketeer Maxie Fields (Walter Matthau), wants to break away from him but doesn't dare.

In an alley outside the school, Danny is jumped by three young hoods led by Shark (Vic Morrow). Against the odds Danny wins the fight and is asked to join up with the trio. He refuses.

Back home Danny's dad (Dean Jagger) announces that, after months out of work, he finally picked up a job in a local drug store and asks Danny to return to school to graduate. Instead, Danny joins Shark and his friends, helping them rob a five and dime store by distracting attention with his singing while the meatheads take the store. A young assistant who works in the store, Nellie (Dolores Hart) sees what's going on, but doesn't tell. Danny makes a date with her.

That night Danny is working in the Blue Shade when Ronnie walks in with Maxie. Danny greets her but, to allay Maxie's suspicions, she pretends not to know him, claiming she only heard him sing once. Maxie challenges Danny to prove he really can sing, which he does. He is then offered a job singing at the King Creole nightclub, owned by Charlie LeGrand (Paul Stewart), the only man on Bourbon Street independent of Maxie.

Danny defies his father, accepts Charlie's offer, becomes a big hit and proceeds to pack the King Creole nightly. Though he is dating Nellie, he has a strong feeling for Ronnie, but she fears Maxie too strongly to do anything about it. Maxie uses Ronnie to force Danny to quit the King Creole to work for him, but Ronnie begs him not to get involved with Maxie. Danny refuses Maxie, so the racketeer calls in Shark to get 'something big' on Danny. This Shark does by involving him in a hold-up at the drug-store where his father works. The hold-up leaves Danny's dad badly hurt.

In a rage Danny gives Maxie a terrible beating. Every hood in town is now after him, and in a showdown with Shark he is knifed. Ronnie takes him to her hideout in the country and nurses him back to health. Maxie tracks them down, kills Ronnie, but then is killed himself by one of his own henchmen whom Danny has befriended.

The movie ends on a bitter/sweet note with Danny returning to his family, the faithful Nellie, and stardom at the King Creole.

King Creole used location shooting for the first time in any of Elvis' films, with New Orleans not unnaturally the selected location. With the Hollywood shooting schedule completed the whole film crew, Elvis and his entourage, assorted hangers-on and the whole crazy circus that was beginning to form around the hottest entertainment property in the land.

The scenes along the route were a carbon copy of those on the journey out to the film capital. Fans lined the tracks at every vantage point, vying for a moment's view of Elvis Presley.

New Orleans went beserk. The city declared the day the crew hit town, an Elvis Presley day, and the children were let off school. The streets were choked with people and filming was difficult. Hal Wallis was amazed. 'I had Dean Martin and Jerry Lewis at their peak and nobody bothered them.' Colonel Parker's answer was typically laconic. 'You've never had Elvis Presley before. You're gonna need extra security.' As was fast becoming standard practise, Elvis took over an entire floor of the Roosevelt Hotel during his stay in New Orleans. The hotel's elevators were rigged to prevent them from stopping at the floor occupied by Elvis and the burgeoning group around him, which the media was starting to tag the Memphis Mafia.

The Memphis Mafia had become Elvis' comfort, his transportable home from home. Although he had become the idol of millions

he had already begun to feel very alone off-stage, and the Mafia became his bit of Tennessee wherever he might actually be. This crew was made up of a group of between seven and twelve guys, all roughly the same age as Elvis, and all with a similar background.

In those early days the Mafia comprised:-

Alan Fortas, who was responsible for traveling arrangements and looking after Elvis' cars.

Sonny West, who helped Alan look after the vehicles and was a native of Memphis. Red West, Sonny's cousin, who'd been a schoolfriend of Presley's back at Humes High, and had been with the King since the very early days.

Elvis' cousins, Gene and Billy (Junior) Smith, who had started touring with him in the Sun era and had grown up with him in Tupelo. Junior took care of Elvis' wardrobe, while Gene simply provided good companionship.

The Mafia was completed by Louis Harris, another native of Memphis and Cliff Gleeves, also a long-standing member of the Presley entourage. Criticism of Elvis' maintenance of this bunch of hangers-on gradually gained momentum, both in the press and among the circle of advisers and well-wishers that surrounded him as his popularity grew.

But they were his roots and his ties and kept him reminded of his home territory and his past. Elvis put it succinctly if less than quite truthfully when he told newsmen: 'I have no need of bodyguards, but I have very specific uses for two highly trained certified public accountants, an expert transportation man to handle travel arrangements, make reservations, take care of baggage, a wardrobe man, a confidential aid, and someone to handle security in large cities where crowds of people are involved. This is my corporation which travels with me at all times. More than that, all these members of my corporation are my friends.'

Monday, March 24, 1958. The weather is cold and wet. Elvis is approaching the local draft office on Main Street, Memphis. As he slows down he turns to his dad sitting in the back seat. 'Looks like the Colonel's got the whole damn show out on the stocks again, pa.'

Vernon Presley nods, looking out the window and catching fifty, sixty reporters waiting for their arrival. Right slap in the middle of this crowd is the ubiquitous Colonel Tom Parker. Carrying brightly colored balloons no less, which read 'See Elvis in *King Creole*.' True to form the Colonel has made a business deal with the Army. If Uncle Sam will allow Elvis' induction to be turned into a publicity jamboree, the Colonel will guarantee that once Elvis is sworn in, the press will leave the Army in peace. The Army went for it, figuring it might as well get all the ballyhoo over with in one day.

Elvis says his goodbyes to his parents and to Judy Spreckels, a friend. They have traveled in the car with him to the draft office, accompanied by Mafia member Lamar Fike who, in a sudden fit of loyalty, claimed he wanted to join the Army with his beloved boss. Lamar's patriotism was cold-shouldered by the draft board; he is grossly overweight.

The other draftees and Elvis are taken to Kennedy Veterans Hospital for their medical. Elvis is photographed at almost every stage of this procedure, to the annoyance of some of the medical fraternity, to the amusement of posterity and some of the others present.

For the afternoon, Colonel Tom has engineered a press conference. Somewhat shyly, Elvis steps before not only news scribes but also a barrage of TV and movie cameras. At the insistence of the Colonel, but with some hesitation, the King reads out a prepared statement but then declines to read any more.

At five o'clock that afternoon Elvis Aaron Presley raises his hand, takes the oath and becomes No. US53310761.

EPILOGUE

The month of August 1958 was the beginning of the end of Elvis Presley. While his parents were still living in Killeen, his mother became 'unable to perform her normal duties'. She lost interest in life, became unsteady on her feet, and found her ability to concentrate faltering.

Elvis drove his mother back to Memphis, where she was admitted to the City's Methodist Hospital.

After three days in hospital, the doctors diagnosed hepatitis, Elvis was contacted in Texas and advised to return home. He was granted emergency leave and, although it was against his nature and his mother's wishes, he flew home — Presley was still very averse to flying at this time. His presence at Gladys' bedside rallied her spirits, but did nothing to improve her physical condition. She remained 'serious' according to hospital jargon, and the end was inevitable.

Elvis, along with his father Vernon, took turns to stay at his mother's bedside, but on August 14, 1958, Gladys Presley died.

The official cause of her death was given as 'heart failure', which may have been technically correct, but which obscured the extent to which her misuse of barbiturates and alcohol had contributed to her early death. Gladys was forty-six, but looked ten years older when she died.

The funeral was to be held in Memphis, and the Blackwood Brothers Quartet were contacted by Vernon Presley to sing at the funeral service. The quartet had been Gladys Presley's favorite group, and they sang *Rock Of Ages*, and Gladys' favorite hymn *Precious Memories*.

J. D. Sumner was a member of the Blackwoods at the time, and he recalled to the author just how shattered Elvis was at the death of his mother. 'Probably more than folks realised at the time, he held his mother in such high esteem, awe and respect. He was completely destroyed.'

Gladys Presley was buried originally at Forest Hills Cemetery just three miles south of Memphis, amongst humble grave markers. At the head of her grave Elvis placed a ten foot marble monument with a life-sized statue of Jesus Christ on the cross with arms outstretched. To his left and right were the fingers of two angels knelt in prayer. At his feet was the simple inscription 'Presley'.

Some while later a normal sized marker was also erected. It read:

GLADYS SMITH PRESLEY
APRIL 25 1912 - AUGUST 14 1958
BELOVED WIFE OF VERNON PRESLEY
AND MOTHER OF ELVIS PRESLEY
'SHE WAS THE SUNSHINE OF OUR HOME'

Elvis stood by his father's side at the funeral service crying, unable to hide his grief. He was heard to mutter 'Oh God, everything I have is gone...'

On that day in August 1958, Elvis Presley, the uninhibited, talented, passionate, original, one-and-only rock 'n' roller...the Tennessee kid who burst out of nowhere to sing the songs that rocked the world....also died.

APPENDIX I
SAM PHILLIPS

A converted radiator repair shop, smaller than the cafe it adjoined, so small in fact that it did not enjoy the luxury of an office, just a small reception area, all the studio equipment hand built, a staff of two, and all the business done in the cafe. Not exactly a promising place to start musical revolutions, but then this is no ordinary address, and this is no ordinary studio: 706 Union Avenue, Memphis, Tennessee.

706 Union Avenue witnessed the discovery of so many of the unique talents of a generation, thanks to the genius of one man, Sam Phillips. Elvis Presley, Jerry Lee Lewis, Carl Perkins and Johnny Cash is a formidable list of protégés by any standards, but before them had come many others such as Howlin' Wolf, B. B. King and Bobby Bland as well as countless sterling, if not legendary, performers like Charlie Rich, Jack Clement, Sleepy La Beef, *et al.*

Was it the fact that Sam Phillips owned the only studio in town that drew all these acts to him? No, that was not the case; there were other studios in Memphis. It was partly Phillips' reputation as a keen-eyed talent spotter, but most of all his willingness to give acts who were different a chance. More than 'willingness', in fact; 'hunger'. Most of the Sun acts approached other studios and had been turned down. Jerry Lee Lewis had been to Nashville and been advised to 'Get himself a guitar'. Sam Phillips took one listen and told Jerry: 'You're a very rich man.'

Maybe no one beyond the confines of Memphis would have heard of Sam Phillips had it not been for Elvis Presley, but then would anyone beyond the confines of Memphis have heard of Elvis Presley had it not been for Sam Phillips? The Sun era as we know it started with Elvis, but Presley was certainly not the beginning of the Sun legend.

Sam Phillips was born in Florence, Alabama on January 5, 1923. Being born in the south, particularly in Alabama, gave the young Phillips a fairly fixed view of life and the role of black people in it, yet black people came to play a crucial part in Phillips' life.

His view modified with the times; thanks to the Depression it became appropriate to judge a person or family on just one thing, income, regardless of color or creed. In post-Depression middle America even if you were white but poor, you were no better than the blacks in some people's eyes.

His earlier aspiration was to be a criminal defense lawyer but instead he went into radio to support his widowed mother. He started at station WLAY in Muscle Shoals as an announcer. It was at this station that he met his wife Becky, who was at the time working as a ukelele player. Phillips went to work as an engineer in Decatur, then at station WREC in Nashville. His arrival in Memphis was at station WREC in 1944. By then Phillips' roots were firmly planted in black music, the music he had been brought up on, and his ambition became to record some of the black singers of the area.

In 1950 he built his own recording studio (the converted radiator shop) and his first recordings were leased out to Chess Records in Chicago. In 1951 he recorded what many people regard as the first-ever genuine rock 'n' roll record, *Rocket 88* by Jackie Brenston, which was released on the Chess label. At the time Phillips was still working for WREC. Six months later he launched his own label, Sun Records, and began recording black artists.

'The negroes had no place to record in the south,' Phillips explains. 'They had to go up to Chicago or New York to get on record and even the most successful of the local entertainers had a hard time doing that. So I set up a studio in 1950 just to make records of those great negro artists.'

Sam Phillips had a great eye, ear and nose for talent but, as he put it, 'I never would fool with anybody who had recorded before I found them.' The first record on the Sun label was never officially released, it was *Blues In My Condition* by Walter 'Shaky' Horton and Jack Kelly. The initial reaction from radio stations who received advance copies was so poor that Phillips withdrew the single. So the first Sun recording that went on general sale

was *Drivin' Slow* by Johnny London, joined almost simultaneously by a single by Walter Bradford called *Dreary Nights*. Neither set the world on fire.

Phillips recorded many singles before Elvis came his way, featuring artists like Little Milton, Billy 'The Kid' Emerson, Howard Seratt, Hardrock Gunter, and two hillbilly acts, Earl Peterson, Michigan's Singing Cowboy and Doug Poindexter and the Starlight Wranglers (the band of which Scotty Moore was a member). Elvis' involvement with Sam Phillips is well covered in this book and elsewhere, but the label's history after Presley is less well-known. Did Sam Phillips ever regret letting Elvis go? 'I must have been asked a thousand times, did I ever regret it? No I did not, I do not, and I never will.'

Sam Phillips began eventually to lose interest in his creation; he found it difficult to compete with the major labels on an honest level, and rather than get into seamier aspects of the fast-growing pop record industry, he quit. He is now a major shareholder in the Holiday Inn chain, and has his own radio station in Memphis.

All the rights to the Sun catalogue were sold to Shelby Singleton, (Elvis' Sun recordings were of course sold to RCA) and much of the catalogue is available in the U.S. on Singleton's Plantation label, and in Britain through Charley Records.

Sam Phillips retains his loyalty to Memphis, still living there in the same house he has inhabited for over twenty years. Credited with starting rock 'n' roll singlehanded, the Phillips myth is perhaps both somewhat exaggerated and simplistic. However, the fact remains that one man and one tiny label had vision at a critical moment — which perhaps would have passed quickly if it had not been nurtured — and rock music is still very much rooted in that old, scratchy Sun catalogue. In the end Phillips stuck to his principles and let the music pass him by.

APPENDIX II
DISCOGRAPHY

The catalogue numbers in this discography are American numbers; where there was a British release that number appears second.

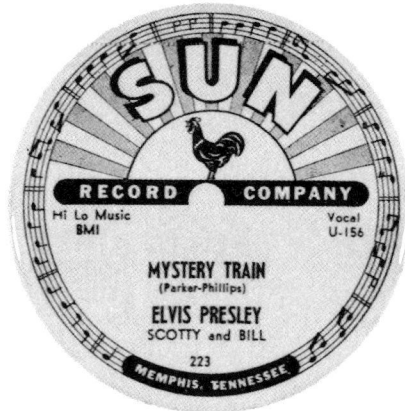

SINGLES

SUN 209   AUG 1954
**That's Alright Mama/
Blue Moon Of Kentucky**

SUN 210   OCT 1954
**Good Rockin' Tonight/
I Don't Care If The Sun
Don't Shine**

SUN 215   JAN 1955
**Milkcow Blues Boogie/
You're A Heartbreaker**

SUN 217   MAY 1955
**I'm Left, You're Right,
She's Gone/Baby Let's Play
House**

SUN 223   AUG 1955
**Mystery Train/
I Forgot To Remember To
Forget**

The above five singles were re-released by RCA Victor in November 1955 on occasion of Elvis signing for the company.

RCA 6420/HMV POP 182
JAN 1956/MAR 1956
**Heartbreak Hotel/
I Was The One**

RCA 6540/HMV POP 235
MAY 1956/JUL 1956
**I Want You, I Need You, I
Love You/
My Baby Left Me**

RCA 6636/HMV POP 213
JUN 1956/SEPT 1956
**Blue Suede Shoes/
Tutti Frutti**

RCA 6604/HMV POP 249
JUL 1956/OCT 1956
**Hound Dog/
Don't Be Cruel**

RCA 6637   SEPT 1956
**I'm Counting On You/
I Gotta Woman**

RCA 6638   SEPT 1956
**I'll Never Let You Go/
I'm Gonna Sit Right Down
And Cry Over You**

RCA 6639   SEPT 1956
**Trying To Get To You/
I Love You Because**

RCA 6640   SEPT 1956
**Blue Moon/
Just Because**

RCA 6641   SEPT 1956
**Money Honey/
One Sided Love Affair**

RCA 6642   SEPT 1956
**Shake Rattle And Roll/
Lawdy Miss Clawdy**

RCA 6643/HMV POP 253
SEPT 1956/DEC 1956
**Love Me Tender/
Anyway You Want Me**

HMV POP 272   NOV 1956
**Blue Moon/I Don't Care If
The Sun Don't Shine**
(BRITISH RELEASE ONLY)

RCA 6800/HMV POP 330
JAN 1957/APR 1957
**Too Much/
Playing For Keeps**

HMV POP 295   FEB 1957
**Love Me/
Mystery Train**
(BRITISH RELEASE ONLY)

HMV POP 305   MAR 1957
**Baby Let's Play House/
Rip It Up**
(BRITISH RELEASE ONLY)

RCA 6870/HMV POP 359
MAR 1957/JUNE 1957
**All Shook Up/
That's When Your
Heartaches Begin**

RCA 7000/RCA 1013
JUN 1957/1957
**Teddy Bear/
Loving You**

HMV POP 378   AUG 1957
**Paralyzed/
When My Blue Moon Turns
To Gold Again**
(BRITISH RELEASE ONLY)

RCA 7035/RCA 1028
SEPT/1957/1958
**Jailhouse Rock/
Treat Me Nice**

HMV POP 408   OCT 1957
**Lawdy Miss Clawdy/
Trying To Get To You**
(BRITISH RELEASE ONLY)

RCA 7150/RCA 1028
DEC 1957/1958
Don't/I Beg Of You

RCA 1020   1957
**Gotta Lotta Livin' To Do/
Praty**
(BRITISH RELEASE ONLY)

RCA 1025   1957
**Santa Bring My Baby Back
To Me/
Santa Claus Is Back In
Town**
(BRITISH RELEASE)

HMV POP 428   JAN 1958
**I'm Left, You're Right,
She's Gone/
How Do You Think I Feel**
(BRITISH RELEASE)

RCA 7240/RCA 1058
APR 1958/1958
**Wear My Ring Around
Your Neck/
Doncha Think It's Time**

RCA 7280/1070
JUN 1958/1958
**Hard Headed Woman/
Don't Ask Me Why**

RCA 1081   1958
**King Creole/
Dixieland Rock**
(BRITISH RELEASE ONLY)

RCA 1088   1958
**All Shook Up/
Heartbreak Hotel**
(BRITISH RELEASE ONLY)

RCA 1095   1958
**Hound Dog/
Blue Suede Shoes**
(BRITISH RELEASE ONLY)

RCA 7410/RCA 1100
OCT 1958/1959
I Got Stung/One Night

EXTENDED PLAY RECORDS

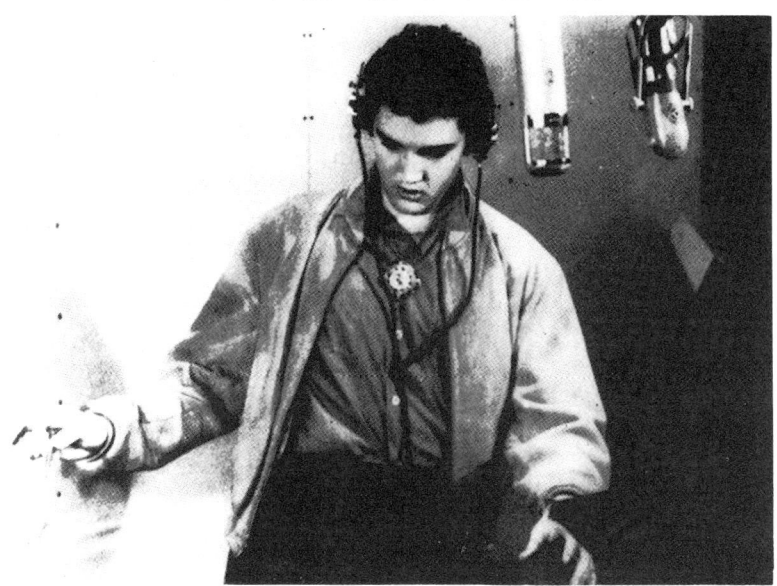

RCA EPB-1254 MAR 1956
ELVIS PRESLEY
(Double E.P.)
Blue Suede Shoes/
I'm Counting On You/
I Gotta Woman/
One Sided Love Affair/
Tutti Frutti/
Trying To Get To You/
I'm Gonna Sit Right Down
And Cry Over You/
I'll Never Let You Go

RCA EPA-747 MAR 1956
ELVIS PRESLEY
Blue Suede Shoes/
Tutti Frutti/
I Gotta Woman/
Just Because

RCA EPA-821 MAY 1956
HEARTBREAK HOTEL
Heartbreak Hotel/
I Was The One/
Money Honey/
I Forgot To Remember To Forget

RCA EPA-830 SEPT 1956
SHAKE RATTLE AND ROLL
Shake Rattle and Roll/
I Love You Because/
Blue Moon/
Lawdy Miss Clawdy

RCA EPA-940 SEPT 1956
THE REAL ELVIS
Don't Be Cruel/
I Want You, I Need You, I Love You/
Hound Dog/
My Baby Left Me

RCA EPA-965 OCT 1956
ANYWAY YOU WANT ME
Anyway You Want Me/
I'm Left, You're Right She's Gone/
I Don't Care If The Sun Don't Shine/
Mystery Train

RCA EPA-992 NOV 1956
ELVIS - VOL.1
Rip It Up/
Love Me/
When My Blue Moon Turns To Gold Again/Paralyzed

RCA EPA-4006/
HMV 7EG 8199
DEC 1956/FEB 1957
LOVE ME TENDER
Love Me Tender/
Let Me/Poor Boy/
We're Gonna Move

RCA EPA-993 DEC 1956
ELVIS - VOL.2
So Glad Your Mine/
Old Shep/
Ready Teddy/
Anyplace Is Paradise

RCA EPA-994 JAN 1957
STRICTLY ELVIS
Long Tall Sally/
First In Line/
How Do You Think I Feel/
How's The World Treating You

RCA EPA-1-1515
JUN 1957
LOVING YOU VOL.1.
Loving You/
Party/Teddy Bear/
True Love

RCA EPA-2-1515
JUN 1957
LOVING YOU VOL.2.
Lonesome Cowboy/
Hot Dog/
Mean Woman Blues/
Got A Lot A'Livin' To Do

RCA-RCX-101   1957
PEACE IN THE VALLEY
(BRITISH RELEASE)
Peace In The Valley/
It Is No Secret/
I Believe/
Take My Hand Precious Lord

HMV 7EG 8256 SEPT 1957
GOOD ROCKING TONIGHT
(BRITISH RELEASE)
Blue Moon Of Kentucky/
Good Rocking Tonight/
Milk Cow Blues/
Just Because

RCA EPA-4041/
RCA RCX-104 SEPT 1957/1957
**JUST FOR YOU/
ELVIS PRESLEY**
I Need You Do/
Blueberry Hill/
Have I Told You Lately That I Love You/
Is It So Strange

RCA EPA-4054 APR 1957
PEACE IN THE VALLEY
Peace In The Valley/
It Is No Secret/
I Believe/
Take My Hand Precious Lord

RCA EPA-4108/RCA RCX-121
NOV 1957/1958
ELVIS SINGS CHRISTMAS SONGS
Santa Bring My Baby Back To Me/
Blue Christmas/
Santa Claus Is Back In Town/
I'll Be Home For Christmas

RCA EPA-4114/RCA RCX-106
NOV 1957/1958
JAILHOUSE ROCK
Jailhouse Rock/
Young And Beautiful/
I Want To Be Free/
Don't Leave Me Now/
Baby I Don't Care

RCA EPA-4319/RCA RCX-117
OCT 1958/1958
KING CREOLE VOL.1.
King Creole/
New Orleans/
As Long As I Have You/
Lover Doll

RCA EPA-4321/RCA RCX118
OCT 1958/1958
KING CREOLE VOL.2.
Trouble/
Young Dreams/
Crawfish/
Dixieland Rock

RCA EPA-4325/RCA RCX-131
MAR 1959/1958
ELVIS SAILS
Press interview with Elvis at Brooklyn Army terminal 22 September 1958: Elvis Presley's newsreel interview/Pat Hernon interviews Elvis in the library of the S. S. Randall.

LONG PLAYING ALBUMS

LPM-1254 APR 1956
ELVIS PRESLEY
Blue Suede Shoes/
I'm Counting On You/
I Gotta Woman/
One Sided Love Affair/
I Love You Because/
Just Because/
Tutti Frutti/
Tryin' To Get To You/
I'm Gonna Sit Right Down And Cry/
I'll Never Let You Go/
Blue Moon/Money Honey

LPM-1382 OCT 1956
ELVIS
Rip It Up/
Love Me/
When My Blue Moon Turns To Gold Again/
Long Tall Sally/
First In Line/
Paralyzed/
So Glad You're Mine/
Old Shep/
Ready Teddy/
Anyplace Is Paradise/
How's The World Treating You/
How Do You Think I Feel

HMV CLP-1093
(BRITISH RELEASE ONLY)
NOV 1956
ROCK 'N' ROLL NO.1
Blue Suede Shoes/
I Gotta Woman/
I'm Counting On You/
I'm Left, You're Right, She's Gone/
That's Alright Mama/
Money Honey/
Mystery Train/
I'm Gonna Sit Right Down And Cry/
Trying To Get To You/
One Sided Love Affair/
Lawdy Miss Clawdy/
Shake Rattle And Roll

HMV CLP-1105
(BRITISH RELEASE ONLY)
APR 1957
ROCK 'N' ROLL NO.2
Rip It Up/
Love Me/
When My Blue Moon Turns To Gold Again/
Long Tall Sally/
First In Line/
Paralyzed/So Glad You're Mine/
Old Shep/
Ready Teddy/
Anyplace Is Paradise/
How's The World Treating You/
How Do You Think I Feel

LPM-1515 JUL 1957
LOVING YOU
Mean Woman Blues/
Teddy Bear/
Loving You/
Got A Lotta' Livin' To Do/
Lonesome Cowboy/
Hot Dog/Party/
Blueberry Hill/
True Love/
Don't Leave Me Now/
Have I Told You Lately That I Love You/I Need You So

HMV DLP-1159 10" LP
(BRITISH RELEASE ONLY)
OCT 1957
THE BEST OF ELVIS
Heartbreak Hotel/
I Don't Care If The Sun Don't Shine/
Blue Moon/
Tutti Frutti/
All Shook Up/
Hound Dog/Too Much/
Anyway You Want Me/Don't Be Cruel/
Playin' For Keeps

RCA RC-24001 10" LP
(BRITISH RELEASE ONLY)
1957
LOVING YOU
Mean Woman Blues/
Teddy Bear/
Loving You/Got A Lot O' Livin' To Do/
Lonesome Cowboy/
Hot Dog/Party/
True Love

RCA LOC-1035/
RCA RD-27052
NOV 1957/1957
ELVIS' CHRISTMAS ALBUM
Santa Claus Is Back In Town/
White Christmas/
Here Comes Santa Claus/
I'll Be Home For Christmas/
Blue Christmas/
Santa Bring My Baby Back/O Little Town Of Bethlehem/
Silent Night/
Peace In The Valley/
I Believe/Take My Hand Precious Lord/
It Is No Secret

RCA LPM-1707
MAR 1958
ELVIS' GOLDEN RECORDS
Hound Dog/
Loving You/
All Shook Up/
Heartbreak Hotel/
Jailhouse Rock/
Love Me/Too Much/
Don't Be Cruel/
That's When Your Heartaches Begin/
Teddy Bear/Love Me Tender/
Treat Me Nice/
Anyway You Want Me/
I Want You, I Need You, I Love You

RCA LPM-1884/RCA 27088
AUG 1958/1958
KING CREOLE
King Creole/
As Long As I Have You/
Hard Headed Woman/
Trouble/
Dixieland Rock/
Don't Ask Me Why/
Lover Doll /Crawfish/
Young Dreams/
Steadfast Loyal And True/New Orleans

RCA RB-16069
(BRITISH RELEASE ONLY) 1958
ELVIS' GOLDEN RECORDS VOL.1
Hound Dog/
I Love You Because/All Shook Up/
Heartbreak Hotel/
You're A Heartbreaker/
Love Me/Too Much/
Don't Be Cruel/
That's When Your Heartaches Begin/
I'll Never Let You Go/Love Me Tender/
I Forgot To Remember To Forget/
Anyway You Want Me/
I Want You, I Need You, I Love You

THE FILMS 1954-1956

LOVE ME TENDER 1956
(Black & White)
20th Century Fox:
Prod. David Weisbart:
Dir. Robert Webb.

LOVING YOU
1957 (Color)
Paramount:
Prod. Hal B. Wallis:
Dir. Hal Kanter.

JAILHOUSE ROCK
1957 (Black & White)
Metro Goldwyn Mayer:
Prod. Pandro S. Berman:
Dir. Richard Thorpe.

KING CREOLE
1958 (Black & White)
Paramount:
Prod. Hal B. Wallis:
Dir. Michael Curtiz.

CHRONOLOGY OF THE LIFE OF ELVIS PRESLEY 1954-1958

1954

January 4: Elvis recorded *Casual Love Affair* and *I'll Never Stand In Your Way* on an acetate at Memphis Recording Service and meets Sam Phillips for the first time.

July 4: Elvis meets Scotty Moore and Bill Black for the first time as they attempt to rehearse at Scotty's house.

July 5: Elvis' first commercial recording session at Sun Records (Memphis Recording Service) where *I Love You Because*, *That's Alright Mama* and *Blue Moon Of Kentucky* are put down.

July 7: Dewey Phillips, a disc jockey on station WHBQ becomes the first DJ to play an Elvis Presley record when he plays *That's Alright Mama* on his *Red, Hot and Blue* program. Later in the same program Elvis gave his first interview.

July 19: Elvis' first commercial single was released coupling *That's Alright Mama* with *Blue Moon Of Kentucky*.

July 30: Elvis made his first proper concert appearance at the Overton Park Shell, Memphis on a bill headed by Slim Whitman.

September 25: Elvis made his first and only appearance on *The Grand Ole Opry* singing *Blue Moon Of Kentucky*. Topping the section of the show in which Elvis performed was Hank Snow. *Good Rockin' Tonight/I Don't Care If The Sun Don't Shine* released.

October 16: Elvis made his first of many appearances on *The Louisiana Hayride* singing *That's Alright Mama*.

1955

January 1: Bob Neal became Elvis' second manager, taking over from Scotty Moore.

January 8: *Milk Cow Blues Boogie/You're A Heartbreaker* released.

April 1: *Baby Let's Play House/I'm Left, You're Right, She's Gone* released.

May 13: Elvis appeared at Jacksonville, Florida and for the first time a personal appearance causes a riot.

May 26: Elvis appears at the Jimmie Rodgers Memorial day celebrations in Meridian, Mississippi.

August 17: *Mystery Train/I Forgot To Remember To Forget* released.

November 22: RCA Records purchase Elvis' contract from Sun Records for $25,000 from which Elvis collected $5,000.

December 17: Elvis made his last appearance on the *Louisiana Hayride*.

1956

January 10: Elvis' first RCA recording session took place at which the first song taped was *I Gotta Woman*.

January 27: *Heartbreak Hotel/I Was The One* released.

January 28: Elvis made his first appearance on National TV on the Dorsey Brothers *Stage Show* on CBS TV.

February 4: The second appearance on *Stage Show*.

February 11: The third appearance on *Stage Show*.

February 18: The fourth appearance on *Stage Show*.

March 15: Colonel Tom Parker became Elvis' official manager.

March 17: The fifth appearance on *Stage Show*.

March 24: The sixth and last appearance on *Stage Show*.

April 1: Elvis made a screen test for Hal Wallis.

April 3rd: First appearance on the *Milton Berle Show*.

April 23rd-29: Elvis made his first appearance in Las Vegas at the New Frontier Hotel, where he gained a poor reception.

June 5: The second appearance on the *Milton Berle Show*.

July 1: Elvis made an appearance on the *Steve Allen Show*.

August 22: Elvis started filming *Love Me Tender*.

September 9: The first appearance on the *Ed Sullivan Show*.

November 16: *Love Me Tender* film released.

1957

January 4: Elvis took his pre-induction Army medical at the Kennedy Veterans Hospital in Memphis.

March 19: Elvis purchased *Graceland* from Mrs Ruth Brown-Moore.

July 9: *Loving You* film released.

October 21: *Jailhouse Rock* film released.

December 20: Elvis received his call up papers for the Army. He is however given a sixty day deferment after his film studio write to the Army requesting time for Elvis to finish the *King Creole* film.

1958

March 24: Elvis inducted into U.S. Army.